WHY>

WITH
JUD WILHITE

PURSUING ANSWERS TO LIFE'S BIGGEST QUESTIONS

Published by Pursuit, Inc.
1001 New Beginnings Drive
Henderson, NV 89011
www.pursuit.org

ISBN 0-9773975-0-5

Cover design and book layout by PlainJoe Studios in Corona, CA.

Printed in Canada
10 9 8 7 6

Introduction

If you've ever been around young children for any length of time, you've probably heard them ask, "Why?" My young daughter, Emma, constantly asks me, "Why Daddy? Why do you have to go to work? Why do I have to go to bed? Why? Why? Why?" The list goes on and on. Sometimes there's even a "Why?" to the "Why?" Though I said I'd never do it, I find myself answering just like my parents, "Because I said so, that's why!"

As we grow older, we find answers to the more simple questions. We know why Dad has to go to work and why we have to go to bed, but we never really grow out of asking why. We're just asking tougher questions, and this time, we're asking God questions like, "Why does bad stuff happen to good people? Why is faith so confusing? Why should I trust the Bible?"

These are all great questions and we'll be looking at their answers and more over the next forty days. This book is designed to help you find answers to the questions you're asking and being asked by others.

To get the most out of your study I encourage you to read only one chapter a day, and spend some time reflecting on what you read. Look up the scripture references and ask God to open your eyes and heart. For further study on any of the topics check out the recommended resources in the back of this book.

God is waiting to show you the answers to life's biggest questions. In the next forty days you'll discover more about your faith than you ever knew possible. Enjoy the pursuit!

Jud Wilhite
Senior Pastor
Central Christian Church
Las Vegas

About the Authors and Editors

Jud Wilhite, Author and Contributing Editor

Jud is the Senior Pastor of Central Christian Church in Las Vegas, NV. Through his leadership, Central has become a pioneering community of faith that has reached in excess of thirteen thousand in attendance. He has authored several books including his latest, *Stripped: Uncensored Grace on the Streets of Vegas*. His message and inspiration to exhibit uncensored grace is found in WHY> and other Pursuit books and resources.

Mike Bodine, Contributing Editor

Mike is the Senior Leader of Central Christian Church in Las Vegas, NV. Through his leadership, Central thrives as a church that reaches and disciples people through radical alignment, a process he and Pursuit call ChurchSync™. ChurchSync™ principles are wired into Pursuit Campaigns and other Pursuit resources and are one of the reasons these materials are so effective at reaching and discipling people.

Bart Rendel, Executive Editor

Bart is the President of Pursuit Ministries. Pursuit grew out of the ministry of Central Christian Church in Las Vegas, NV and exists to help other churches respond to the Great Commission by teaching and resourcing them in the principles of uncensored grace and radical alignment. Bart is also the Executive Editor of the WHY> campaign, book, and equipping materials.

The Pursuit Team, Authors

A great portion of this book was written by a talented team of authors whose passion is to see people equipped to defend their faith or get answers to their most burning spiritual questions. The Pursuit Team has written several other books and studies dedicated to reaching people and teaching them about the life-changing and practical truths of Scripture. Look for more life-transformational studies and resources at www.pursuit.org.

TABLE OF CONTENTS

QUESTION 1>

WHY AM I HERE?

Life is a pursuit, a journey full of discovery. People are on all kinds of pursuits today. Some are pursuing a dream, others a relationship, and some are pursuing happiness or money. What you seek reflects what you desire. Jesus said, "For where your treasure is, there your heart will be also" (Matthew 6:21, ESV). What are you pursuing? How does God fit into it? What does it mean to seek God with all of your heart, and why does life so often hinder that pursuit?

Whether you're a deeply committed follower of Christ or someone just beginning a spiritual journey, the next forty days are designed to help you know and treasure Jesus more. This first week we'll discover who is really seeking answers to life's biggest questions and just what life's most important question is.

We Seek God
Many people seek God or at least something spiritual. Recently celebrities have been practicing Kabbalah and Scientology, which are just two of the seemingly endless string of differing religions and faiths that people seek.

The Bible says if we seek God, we will find Him. Here are just a few examples.

> My son, if you receive my words and treasure up my commandments with you, making your ear attentive to wisdom and inclining your heart to understanding; yes, if you call out for insight and raise your voice for understanding, if you **seek** it like silver and search for it as for hidden treasures, then you will understand the fear of the LORD and find the knowledge of God (Proverbs 2:1-5, ESV).

> But **seek** first the kingdom of God and his righteousness, and all these things will be added to you (Matthew 6:33, ESV).

> Ask, and it will be given to you; **seek**, and you will find; knock, and it will be opened to you. For everyone who asks receives, and the one who **seeks** finds, and to the one who knocks it will be opened (Matthew 7:7-8, ESV).

God is ready and willing to give you answers about who He is and why He created you. All you have to do is ask and seek Him.

God Seeks Us

Believe it or not, we're not the only ones searching. God is seeking us out too. "But the hour is coming, and is now here, when the true worshipers will worship the Father in spirit and truth, for the Father is **seeking** such people to worship him. God is spirit, and those who worship him must worship in spirit and truth" (John 4:23-24, ESV).

These verses are part of a conversation Jesus had with a woman in Samaria. Jesus' encounter with this Samaritan woman (John 4:7-30) gives us insight into the heart of God and the process of seeking Him. So let's take a closer look.

Jesus was journeying with His disciples from Galilee to Jerusalem. For most Jews, that meant traveling an indirect route to avoid passing through Samaria because tension between Jews and Samaritans had existed for centuries. So when Jesus asks a Samaritan woman for a drink, she is completely caught off guard.

John 4:7-9 says, "When a Samaritan woman came to draw water, Jesus said to her, 'Will you give me a drink?' (His disciples had gone into the town to buy food). The Samaritan woman said to Him, 'You are a Jew and I am a Samaritan woman. How can you ask me for a drink?' (For Jews do not associate with Samaritans.)"

Jesus violates a number of cultural taboos here—first He speaks to a woman in public. In Jesus' day, men did not do this. It is also likely that the woman is an outcast since she came to draw water from the well alone. Customarily women went to the well together for small talk and to draw water for the next day's supply. The biggest problem, however, is stated by the woman in verse nine when she says Jews and Samaritans do not mix, and they do not drink from one another's cup. Nevertheless, Jesus engages her in conversation by asking her for some water.

Clearly this woman of Samaria had no special intentions. She was just coming to draw water. Yet, on this day, she enters into a conversation with Jesus that changes her life. Jesus, on the other hand, is thirsty. He has traveled a long distance, and the disciples left Him to buy food in town. He knows there's a deeper need in this woman than physical water—a need she may not even be aware of yet. He seeks to fill that need.

It only makes sense that we want to seek God. After all, He is the creator and God of the universe. But can you imagine Him seeking you and wanting to meet your every need?

Point to Ponder: God is seeking those who are at some level seeking Him.

Question to Consider: How important is it for you to seek God?

When you think of water, what comes to mind? The list might include the beach, bottled drinking water, floods, fishing, or waterskiing. Estimates vary, but somewhere between 70 and 75 percent of the earth's surface is covered with water. Water is necessary for life. In some organisms, up to 90 percent of their body weight comes from water. Up to 60 percent of the human body is water: your brain is 70 percent water, blood is 82 percent water, and the lungs are nearly 90 percent water.

Yesterday we looked at the story of Jesus and the woman of Samaria (John 4). Remember how she was totally caught off guard by Jesus' request for water? She reminded Him that Jews and Samaritans do not drink from the same cup. Interestingly, we're never told whether or not Jesus actually drinks water from her cup. This is probably because Jesus' thirst goes beyond water; He's more concerned for this woman than His own basic needs.

"Jesus answered her, 'If you knew the gift of God and who it is that asks you for a drink, you would have asked him and he would have given you living water" (John 4:10).

Living water, what is that? Maybe Jesus was thinking about the Old Testament prophets.

"They will neither hunger nor thirst, nor will the desert heat or the sun beat upon them. He who has compassion on them will guide them and lead them beside springs of water" (Isaiah 49:10, NIV).

"My people have committed two sins: They have forsaken me, the spring of living water, and have dug their own cisterns, broken cisterns that cannot hold water" (Jeremiah 2:13, NIV).

The living water Jesus offers to the woman is a metaphor for God and the life He offers. It's the water of life that quenches the parched lips of the thirsty. Her response, however, tells us she doesn't yet understand.

"Sir,' the woman said, 'you have nothing to draw with and the well is deep. Where can you get this living water? Are you greater than our father, Jacob, who gave us the well and drank from it himself, as did also his sons and his flocks and herds?'" (John 4:11-12, NIV).

The woman is perplexed. Wouldn't you be? Here is this man, a Jew, asking a Samaritan woman for a drink of water, and then He offers this thing called living water. She's beginning to sense something and wonders if this man is different. Is He greater than Father Jacob who provided the well? When Jesus senses her interest He says, "Everyone who drinks this water [from the well] will be thirsty again, but whoever drinks the water I give him will never thirst. Indeed, the water I give him will become in him a spring of water welling up to eternal life" (John 4:13-14).

Well, there it is; this is no ordinary water. This water quenches the thirsty and brings eternal life. She wants this water. "The woman said to him, 'Sir, give me this water so that I won't get thirsty and have to keep coming here to draw water'" (John 4:15). She's not exactly sure what this water is all about. Does it have special powers? Does it cost anything? Whatever it is, she wants it.

We Can Seek Others

It's important to look at what Jesus does here. He doesn't wear a sandwich board proclaiming He is the Messiah. He doesn't condemn the woman for her sins. He relates to a common need—the need for water. He meets her right where He finds her and uses questions to engage her interest.

We live in a land of spiritually thirsty people. They're our friends, neighbors, coworkers, and family. Like Jesus, we can seek them out by asking them questions and relating to their everyday needs and concerns. Consider who that might be in your world today.

As you do, remember the old adage, "You can lead a horse to water, but you can't make him drink." So don't force people into something they don't want to do or pressure them to make a decision. Simply guide them along their path to God. Jesus said, "You are the salt of the earth" (Matthew 5:13). So throw a little salt in their water and make them thirsty.

Point to Ponder: Jesus said, "You are the salt of the earth... [and] the light of the world" (Matthew 5:13-14). Salt preserves and light illuminates. The only sandwich board people should see is you pointing to Jesus.

Question to Consider: Is there someone in your life who is spiritually thirsty? Someone you can point toward Jesus?

Have you ever stood in the candy aisle of a grocery store, looking at all the choices, and had a hard time picking the one you wanted? I sure have. We live in a world of choices, and spiritual choices are just as varied as anything else on the market. They seem endless. The gods of our age can be sampled at just about any local bookstore.

I was recently in Barnes & Noble and came across a display table advertising just such a spiritual menu. The books ranged from witchcraft, Jewish mysticism, and *The Book of Mormon* to biographies of the Apostle Paul and Jesus. All this variety reflects spiritual hunger in a buffet of choices.

Yesterday we left Jesus and the woman of Samaria discussing living water. When offered the water, the woman didn't hesitate to respond to Jesus. In fact, she commanded Jesus, saying, "Give me this water" (John 4:15). She thought Jesus was talking about physical water. At this point in the conversation, Jesus begins to probe into the woman's life at a deeper level. He says, "Go, call your husband and come back" (verse 16). Now, you might wonder why He said this. Jesus already knows what she's going to say, but He also knows what she needs and He wants to help. Her response reveals just how deep that need goes.

"I have no husband," she replied (verse 17).

"Jesus said to her, 'You are right when you say you have no husband. The fact is, you have had five husbands, and the man you now have is not your husband. What you have just said is quite true'" (verses 17-18).

Do you think she's trying to avoid Jesus' request by saying, "I have no husband"? Or is she just being honest? It was true she had no husband. Jewish custom limited marriage to three tries before one became utterly suspect in the culture. Living with someone other than your spouse made you ceremonially unclean and one to be avoided. Jesus ignores these cultural and religious standards and commends her honesty. It must have been strange for her to go draw water in the middle of the day, hoping to avoid human contact, and then bump into someone she'd never met, but who knows her past. Her response is amusing. "'Sir,' the woman said, 'I can see that you are a prophet' (verse 19).

If she wasn't involved in the conversation before, she sure is now. Jesus knows her story, yet they've never met. The truth is, Jesus knows all of our stories. He knows our deepest secrets and our worst faults. But like this woman, He sees beyond the sin in us and stretches out His hand of love to offer us a whole new way of living; a life of forgiveness and acceptance. This is the Gospel—the Good News—something to be heralded, announced, and proclaimed. It's the greatest news flash in human history. The God of all creation has descended to our world, not to condemn us, but to love us.

Isaiah, the prophet, envisioned it this way: "The people walking in darkness have seen a great light; on those living in the land of the shadow of death a light has dawned" (Isaiah 9:2). Jesus is the light. He illuminates the darkness of every life willing to turn to Him. That was His purpose in coming to earth—to seek and save what was lost (Luke 19:10).
We all know people walking in darkness. People who are ashamed, confused, and lost. People like this woman of Samaria. People who thirst, but haven't discovered the real fountain of life. Like her, they may know some things about Jesus, and they may even think of Him as a prophet or famous religious leader. Everyone has an opinion about Jesus.

Her challenge is everyone's challenge—to go beyond our opinions of Jesus, drop to our knees and surrender our lives to Him. Remember His words, "Whoever drinks the water I give him will never thirst. Indeed, the water I give him will become in him a spring of water welling up to eternal life" (John 4:14).

The pursuit doesn't end at the moment of surrender. It must begin there. It continues as we learn about and treasure God more everyday. Jesus put it this way: "Now this is eternal life: that they may know you, the only true God, and Jesus Christ, whom you have sent" (John 17:3). This is Jesus' desire for you whether you're a deeply committed follower of Christ or someone just beginning a spiritual journey. His offer is clear and the choice is yours.

Point to Ponder: God's love for you flows from who He is, not who you are. Jesus made God's love known to those shut out by the religious leaders of His day. His love and acceptance is still reaching out to the outcasts of our day.

Question to Consider: To what degree have you accepted the love of God offered to you in the form of Jesus Christ?

Have you ever asked a question you later regretted asking? Maybe your question and the discussion that followed led down a path you didn't intend it to, or it exposed a faulty idea. I remember more than once asking a question that revealed my ignorance in a class. Does this mean we shouldn't ask questions? No, but some questions are just better left unasked. However, this isn't the case with the woman of Samaria; she asks Jesus a question that changes everything.

She thinks Jesus is a prophet, and like other spiritual seekers, she begins to change the subject from her life to a question she pursues. She wonders, "Well, tell me this: Our ancestors worshiped God at this mountain, but you Jews insist that Jerusalem is the only place for worship, right?" (John 4:20, MSG). Just as in our times, religious conflict and controversy swirled in first-century Palestine. The Samaritans built their own temple to worship God in the city of Gerizim four hundred years earlier, and they rejected the Jerusalem temple as the place of worship. This caused great dissension between Jews and Samaritans. The Samaritan woman is reminding Jesus that she's an outcast because of her shady past and Samaritan heritage. Jesus shows by His response that questions deserve answers.

Answering clearly and directly, "Jesus declared, 'Believe me, woman, a time is coming when you will worship the Father neither on this mountain nor in Jerusalem. You Samaritans worship what you do not know; we worship what we do know, for salvation is from the Jews. Yet a time is coming and has now come when the true worshipers will worship the Father in spirit and truth, for they are the kind of worshipers the Father seeks. God is spirit, and his worshipers must worship in spirit and in truth'" (John 4:21-24).

Jesus quickly acknowledges the ignorance of Samaritan claims, but provides a lane of hope to travel on. He says the place of worship is changing; it's no longer on this mountain or in the city of Jerusalem. It has more to do with the heart than the location. He instructs her about the true nature of worship. God is seeking people who worship from the heart in spirit and truth. The past controversy between Samaritans and Jews is not relevant. A new day is here.

This unexpected answer piques her curiosity even more. The woman replies, "I know that Messiah [called Christ] is coming. When he comes, he will explain everything to us" (John 4:25). She's obviously looking for answers and expects to get them when the Messiah comes. Without hesitation Jesus declares, "I who speak to you am he" (John 4:26). Jesus extends an invitation directly to this woman. He's rarely this candid in any of the other Gospels. If we were to interpret this invitation, it may sound like the words from the Gospel of Matthew where Jesus said, "Come to me, all you who are weary and burdened, and I will give you rest. Take my yoke upon you and learn from me, for I am gentle and humble in heart, and you will find rest for your souls. For my yoke is easy and my burden is light" (Matthew 11:28-30).

The Samaritan woman progresses from seeing Jesus as a Jewish stranger to seeing Him as a prophet, and is now beginning to wonder if He really is the long-awaited Messiah. He began with a request for water, and the conversation led to a spiritual question about worship. Questions are inevitable when talking with people about spiritual matters. Jesus continually answered and raised questions during His time on earth. He valued honest questions. In fact, questions can demonstrate genuine spiritual interest.

So why are we so intimidated by questions? Are we afraid we may not know the answers? It's only natural to be a little nervous when asked questions that carry so much weight; even people who are experienced in answering questions of faith can be intimidated by spiritual challenges. However, there's good news—the same questions get asked all the time. After all, there are only so many inquiries to be made.

In the coming weeks, we'll consider five of the questions most frequently asked by spiritual seekers. No matter where you are in your spiritual pursuit, you'll find some help along the way.

Point to Ponder: Coming to faith in Jesus Christ is a process that takes time. Questions are a welcome companion along that journey.

Question to Consider: How confident are you in your ability to answer the questions that spiritual seekers are asking?

One of life's most important questions is, "Who is Jesus?" Do you know the answer? Is He the Savior of the world? It's certainly worth finding out.

Yesterday we read that Jesus declared to a social outcast that He was the long-awaited Messiah (John 4:26). He offered this news to her without her even asking. As Jesus finished speaking to the woman, His disciples returned and found Him where they had left Him. John records: "Just then his disciples came back. They marveled that he was talking with a woman, but no one said, 'What do you seek?' or, 'Why are you talking with her?'" (John 4:27, ESV).

As we discussed earlier, Jesus broke all social norms by interacting with the woman of Samaria. His disciples were amazed that He spent the whole time speaking with her. Didn't He realize that Jewish laws prohibited a man from speaking with his *wife* in public, let alone a vile Samaritan woman?

The woman wasted no time with her new discovery. John wrote, "So the woman left her water jar and went away into town" (John 4:28, ESV). She had come to fill her water jar before Jesus interrupted her and asked her for a drink. But she left it behind as she rushed into town. She normally would have returned quietly, not wanting to be noticed, but on that day she went public with her newsflash: "'Come, see a man who told me all that I ever did. Can this be the Christ?' They went out of the town and were coming to him" (John 4:29-30 ESV).

Jesus sought her and then she began her own quest. She invited the whole town to join her on this quest—to come and see. She began the journey of faith in Jesus as the Messiah. This is a process that leads down the road of discovery and commitment. She reasoned, "Can it really be true that Jesus is the one sent from God? In my town? At my well? It's too good to be true! Come and see, help me understand what all this means." Real faith is a process; it doesn't occur instantly. It begins with an initial discovery that builds on greater and greater degrees of commitment and surrender. Even though we don't know exactly where this woman is in the process, we know she invites others to come and join her on the quest.

We're told: "Many Samaritans from that town believed in him because of the woman's testimony, 'He told me all that I ever did.' So when the Samaritans came to him, they asked him to stay with them, and he stayed there two days. And many more believed because of his word. They said to the woman, 'It is no longer because of what you said that we believe, for we have heard for ourselves, and we know that this is indeed the Savior of the world'" (John 4:39-42, ESV). A single conversation with Jesus produced a small-scale revival. The Samaritans were as impressed with Jesus as the woman had been. They believed her testimony and pursued Jesus even more, inviting Him to come and stay with them.

It was during these two days that many Samaritans discovered what the woman heard and understood. They too believed because of Jesus' words. They acknowledged Him as the Savior of the world. He was more than just the Messiah of Israel. They understood Him to be the very one that Isaiah, the prophet, revealed, "'You are my witnesses,' declares the LORD, 'and my servant whom I have chosen, so that you may know and believe me and understand that I am he. Before me no god was formed, nor will there be one after me. I, even I, am the LORD, and apart from me there is no savior'" (Isaiah 43:10-11). The seekers in Samaria recognized the one and only Savior, having heard for themselves.

As followers of Christ, we can point people to Jesus, but everyone must eventually come to grips with His claims on their own. They must embrace His words and decide whether He is indeed the Savior of the world. Where are you in that process? Is He the Christ? Is He your Savior?

Point to Ponder: The most important question every person must answer is, "Who is Jesus and how will I respond to Him?"

Question to Consider: How are you currently answering that question?

Life is sometimes so busy that we miss opportunities to share the love of Christ. We're too wrapped up in our own needs to notice anyone else's. Can you imagine what would have happened if Jesus had just taken a drink of water and sat down until the disciples got back? The whole town of Sychar would have missed the Good News.

When the disciples returned, the Samaritan woman went into town to invite all the people to come hear Jesus. Like overly concerned mothers, the disciples urged Jesus to eat (John 4:31). They thought the purpose of coming to Sychar was to buy food. It was supposed to be a quick stop along the journey, and there was no time to waste because they needed to make it to their destination.

Jesus' response must have blown them away. He said, "I have food to eat that you know nothing about" (John 4:32). What did He mean? "Then his disciples said to each other, 'Could someone have brought him food?'" (John 4:33). Their lack of understanding opens the door for Jesus to clarify what He said. "'My food,' said Jesus, 'is to do the will of him who sent me and to finish his work'" (John 4:34). Jesus' overriding passion and life's work was to complete the will of God and to finish God's work. When He said this, He may have been looking ahead in His life to one of His final prayers on earth when He declared, "I have brought you glory on earth by *completing the work* you gave me to do" (John 17:4). Or even further down the road to some of His last words before His death on the cross, "It is finished" (John 19:30). His food is summed up in our memory verse this week, "For the Son of Man came to seek and to save what was lost" (Luke 19:10).

The disciples are obviously focused on the immediate need of the day: food. They want to know, "What's for dinner?" They're wandering through life unaware of the spiritual opportunities around them. We, like them, can learn so much from Jesus.

Jesus approached life with a passion to obey God. He lived with a laser-like focus. There's urgency to His words. His delight is to do God's will. Although He's thirsty and tired, Jesus spent time participating in the most meaningful conversation the woman of Samaria ever had. The most important food we all eat is doing the will of God in our lives. What's your hunger level for this feast?

Jesus urges His disciples, "Do you not say, 'Four months more and then the harvest?' I tell you, open your eyes and look at the fields! They are ripe for harvest. Even now the reaper draws his wages, even now he harvests the crop for eternal life, so that the sower and the reaper may be glad together. Thus the saying 'One sows and another reaps' is true. I sent you to reap what you have not worked for. Others have done the hard work, and you have reaped the benefits of their labor" (John 4:35-38).

Jesus is telling His disciples, "Look up. Open your eyes. There are people all around you who are hungering for spiritual truth, and they're ripe for conversations." The town of Sychar is coming out to meet them; a spiritual harvest is headed their way. For the next two days, Jesus and His disciples minister to the town of thirsty Samaritans. They reaped in a field they hadn't prepared. Those fields are all around us, too. Jesus urges us to simply have a conversation with people about the greatest news flash in human history, and to tell them there is a God who created the universe and He is in hot pursuit of people who are lost. His arms are wide open to them. His pursuit is not to condemn, but rather to forgive and save.

If you opened your eyes and looked up, who would you find with spiritual hunger? Can you have a spiritual conversation with them? Pray and ask God to help them see that He's the only one who can quench the thirst in their souls. Do you wonder, "What if they ask me something I cannot answer?" If so, the remaining weeks will help you focus on the kinds of questions spiritual seekers are asking about Christianity and the answers to the biggest questions of life. Jesus invited us all to be a part of the feast He has prepared. He's now asking us to join Him in inviting others—all we have to do is look up!

Point to Ponder: One of the most significant things you can do in your life is point people to Jesus. You begin by praying for those people and relating to them in everyday life.

Question to Consider: Who could you significantly influence for Jesus Christ? Pray for them daily.

THE SEEKER

by Jud Wilhite
with Bill Taaffe

He was the ultimate Mormon in a sea of Mormons.

He had studied *The Book of Mormon*, *The Doctrine and Covenants*, and *The Pearl of Great Price*—the three great books that define the Mormon faith. He was comfortable in his belief. He was zealous for future converts. And at eighteen years old, Kyle Costello of Ely, Nevada, was about to embark on a two-year mission that male members of the Church of Jesus Christ of Latter-Day Saints are required to serve.

Mormonism ran through Kyle's bloodlines. His forebears, converted during a missionary trip to Europe, had come by ship to New Orleans during the days of Brigham Young and, in an epic journey, pushed a handcart across the Midwest plains to Utah.

Somewhere in those hearty genes was a thirst for rationalism. Kyle wanted to be able to explain to future converts why Mormonism was absolutely true. After all, it seemed only natural that he investigate his own faith thoroughly before he started sharing it with others.

So before leaving on his mission trip to an unknown destination in America or overseas, he set out to answer age-old questions he would surely hear: Don't Mormons practice polygamy? Isn't there racial discrimination among Mormons? Are Mormons really Christians? No way was Kyle going to be out on the mission trail knocking on doors unprepared.

His first stop was his dad, an L.D.S. seminary teacher and member of the elders' quorum. Kyle's dad suggested they meet with his grandfather, a Mormon bishop. Kyle loves and respects both men. But to his surprise they were put off by his questioning. Reluctant to address the subjects he raised, they wondered why he would even dare consider them.

That was not the position to take with Kyle—he of the searching, logical, systematic mind.

It made him question Mormonism for the first time.

Why?

Maybe there was a *reason* they didn't want him to ask these questions.

He set about comparing the teachings of the Bible with those of the three great books of Mormonism. What he found was disconcerting. He discovered huge discrepancies between the Bible (Mormons use only the King James Version) and the great books of Mormonism—discrepancies in how Jesus was viewed and portrayed.

The experience led Kyle to step back and hone in on who Jesus is, as written in the four Gospels of the Bible.

"And more than anything," Kyle says, "I found that this wasn't the Jesus I was taught to know while I was being raised."

Mormonism wasn't about Jesus and His life. It was about what the Mormon prophets told you it was about—Temple marriage, which Jesus never discussed, and becoming a god of one's own world, which has nothing to do with Jesus' message.

As Kyle says: "It was about keeping all these little neatnik laws. And here I saw Jesus in the New Testament saying that His whole thing was a reaction against the Pharisees and their neatnik laws and their attempt to draw boxes around who God was."

So Kyle took a difficult but, in his mind, indispensable step. "I approached my father and said, 'Dad, I want out. I don't want to be part of this faith anymore.' "

There would be no mission trip. And for three years there would be no church of any kind. And there was the sadness that breaches create.

"He was wounded," Kyle says of his dad. "If I put myself in his shoes and my son came to me and told me he was leaving the faith we both shared, I would be extremely wounded too."

As far as Kyle was concerned by now, man had screwed up religion so badly that there was no determining fact from fiction.

He wanted truth, but he didn't find it in his church. He had spent eighteen years of his life, a lot of time and heart and spiritual effort, and seen it crumble. It was like being on an ice floe. One moment he was with his family. Then came a deep-seated crack, and soon he had drifted out to sea.

He was attending college now at the University of Nevada–Las Vegas. And the freedom of agnosticism wasn't so luxurious after all. It was just that he thought of evangelical Christianity as "Christian lite." For him, Christianity was the province of Jim Bakker and

Tammy Faye, Jimmy Swaggart and Benny Hinn—and Pat Robertson, who was running for president at the time.

His view of redemption in born-again Christianity was cynical: "You say this neatnik prayer and then you're fine." At least the Catholics went through rituals. He thought, "If you believe that you just say this prayer and you're saved, you're crazy."

One night he went to dinner with some college friends. He hitched a ride home with a girl in the group. He noticed that her car had a fish symbol on the back. She had struck him as different—intelligent but fun, connected to both friends and family. He knew what the fish meant, but pinned her down anyway.

"So you're a Christian," he said. "Tell me what that means."

"So she tells me in very humble terms," he recalls. "It was her testimony of what Jesus Christ means in her life. I remember being taken aback by how simple and true and honest it was. Very disarming. Plus, she had this life that kind of backed it up."

The girl's name was Joy. They began spending time together, and some months later she invited him to her church.

He wound up disarmed by a part of the pastor's message: "Hey, folks, I'm a messed-up guy. Every day I submit myself to God, but at the end of the day it's not about me. It's about Jesus. It's about following His call for all of us."

For the first time Kyle thought, "Maybe this is a little bit different. I probably should at least give this a whirl."

Kyle jumped back into the Bible as never before, though he had spent two years studying the Old and New Testaments for his mission. He knew the teachings of both testaments cold; what he didn't know were their origins.

One of the articles of Mormon practice is: "We believe the Bible to be the word of God as far as it is translated correctly." Mormons believe that so many translation errors have crept into the Bible over the centuries that certain parts have been removed or added to promote an apostate church.

So Kyle, ever the challenger, decided that if the Christian scriptures could stand his systematic, rigorous test for authenticity, he would believe. If not, he would move on. He wasn't about to accept pat answers this time. He decided to examine the underpinnings of Christianity just the way he recently had done with Mormonism.

The question for him was: "Why?"

It was the ultimate question, asked by less than ten percent of people who ever accept the teachings of Christianity.

Why can the Bible be believed?

Why is it true?

Kyle had always believed that the Bible was somewhat incorrect because it was handed down, handed down, and handed down—obviously subject to an abundance of transcription errors.

In his search, however, he learned that the Bible is *the most* historically backed-up book from the ancient world—both inside and outside religious writings. All ancient scholars, secular and religious, agree. There is no serious debate about the authenticity of the earliest manuscripts that have come down to us.

Kyle investigated the significance of the Dead Sea Scrolls, ancient biblical manuscripts from 250 BC to AD 68 that were found in a cave twenty miles from Jerusalem in 1947. The discovery made worldwide news because it showed that the most venerable Old Testament Scriptures today are ninety-nine percent accurate.

As for the New Testament, he examined support for the oldest texts we have today. He found that they are far more accurate and better corroborated than any other ancient writing of any kind—including Homer's *Iliad* and *Odyssey*, and that of the Jewish historian Josephus.

"I got to the point where I realized the Bible *had* to be supernatural—that there had to be a supernatural hand over it because the evidence for it was so overwhelming," Kyle says. "It wouldn't happen in the normal course of events. But it had happened here."

Today Kyle Costello is married to Joy, the girl with the fish symbol on the back of her car, the girl with the life that Kyle had noticed mirrored her name. He is a Christian minister with an outreach to young couples. His father, now a Mormon bishop himself, has visited Kyle's church.

Kyle has been through an extraordinary journey to the roots of Christianity. And he is more alive than ever before in his thirty years.

It all started with a fundamental question: *Why?*

QUESTION 2>

"I didn't see any God out there."
-Yuri Gagarin, Soviet cosmonaut, after orbiting the earth

Remember the time you stretched out under the stars and gazed into the vast expanse of twinkling galaxies and infinite possibilities? As you contemplated the universe and drank in the amazing night sky, a question welled up in your heart: "God, are you out there?"

Perhaps there was a time of trauma—maybe in a hospital waiting room or after hearing the finality of the word *divorce*. Or it may have been when you faced a life-altering decision. Do you remember taking a step back and crying out in your heart: "God, are you out there?"

If you've ever asked this question, you're in good company. Men and women like you have always questioned the existence of God. Every culture shows evidence of some form of religious activity. All societies have a system of beliefs that acknowledge a higher power. The ancient world practiced religion. Archeologists around the globe have discovered relics of fertility gods and idol worship. Temples and altars have been unearthed that reveal a dependence on numerous supreme beings. The Nile River, frogs, and even the Pharaoh were all respected as deities in Egypt; the plagues of Moses were all in direct response to the worship of them.

When the Apostle Paul visited Mars Hill in Athens, a place of intellectual discussion and dialogue, he noted the many gods displayed around the city. You've probably heard of Zeus, the Greeks' principal ruler of the heavens, but the Greeks also worshiped many other gods. They even erected a shrine to an unknown god in case they missed one. Paul used this as an opportunity to direct their attention to the existence of the true God of creation.

"Men of Athens! I see that in every way you are very religious. For as I walked around and looked carefully at your objects of worship, I even found an altar with this inscription: TO AN UNKNOWN GOD. Now what you worship as something unknown I am going to proclaim to you" (Acts 17:22-23).

Today, people all around the world continue to seek and believe in a higher power. Hinduism and Buddhism permeate the east. Catholicism has been practiced in Western Europe for centuries. Faithful Orthodox Jews still pray at the western wall of Jerusalem. America is full of churches and religions. Though all of these religions are vastly different, the majority of people around the world agree that there is a power above us. They all bow to a cosmic Someone—a supernatural power greater than us.

Does God really exist? Just because temples are raised to various deities doesn't mean there are actually deities out there. Likewise, just because man raises the question of God's existence doesn't mean God is really there. Is a higher power a figment of man's imagination created to fill a void? Has man created God to identify a purpose or find help beyond himself? Is the search for spiritual truth programmed into man like the desire to be loved or the need for community?

One recent study on that question is molecular biologist Dean Hamer's book, *The God Gene: How Faith is Hardwired into Our Genes*. He proposes that people's belief in the existence of God is a matter of their DNA. It's as if something inside of us propels us to find our spiritual Creator.

Solomon said, "He [God] has also set eternity in the hearts of men; yet they cannot fathom what God has done from beginning to end" (Ecclesiastes 3:11). Built into each of us is a sense of eternity. Deep inside of you is an awareness of something more to your existence and someone bigger than you. Whether it's chemical or spiritual is not the issue. The issue is, "God, are you out there?"

God placed within you a need to know. It's like a voice calling out into the darkness before taking the next step. It's normal and natural for you to ask: "Are you there? Can I know you? Can you help me? Can I trust you?"

God wants you to ask questions. He does not call you to **blind faith**, which raises no issues and naively steps into the unknown. Consequently, blind faith can be wrong and lead to destruction. Never leave your brain at the door when it comes to relating to God. You only put yourself at risk for false expectations and major disappointments.

Test, probe, and study the evidence for yourself. God calls you to a **reasonable faith**. "'Come now, let us reason together,' says the Lord" (Isaiah 1:18). If God does exist, then there's no threat to Him in examining His reality. Honest research will not jeopardize His existence. It will only strengthen your faith—your **reasonable faith**—so go ahead and ask it again: "God, are you out there?"

Point to Ponder: You are wired to ask the question, "God, are you out there?" Built into you is a desire to discover and know God.

Question to Consider: When have you wondered whether or not God exists?

WHAT'S YOUR TAKE ON GOD?

"I do not believe in God because I don't believe in Mother Goose."
-Clarence Darrow, 1930

The snow gently drifted through the wintry sky—a perfect setting for Christmas Eve. With the kids bundled in the car, the family set off to discover the dazzling neighborhoods that displayed Christmas cheer with brightly lit rooftops and colorful figurines of reindeers and candy canes. Sometimes the manger scene had center stage on the porch or front yard, but clearly it was Santa who captivated the attention of the holiday celebration.

This particular evening, the trip around town was part of a ploy. While the children were gone, *you know who* was back at the ranch. When the happy family returned, lo and behold, there in the window standing in front of the Christmas tree, was a man in a red suit. The kids screamed with delight and shouted wildly, "It's Santa! It's Santa!"

Dad ran into the house and chased the merry intruder out the back door. When he returned, Dad had a black boot in his hand. The children's eyes were wide as they touched the boot of old Saint Nick. One of them started to cry because he was worried Santa would catch cold without it. Dad assured him that Santa always carried a spare, and all the while no one noticed that Uncle Joe was nowhere to be seen that evening.

Parents sometimes go to great lengths to convince their children that Santa Claus is real. Truth be told, the jolly old soul is a tale of folklore—a fictitious character made up to further holiday cheer. True Santa believers could build a case for the existence of him, especially if they still had a boot as evidence, but they would be wrong. In reality, he doesn't exist.

But what about God? Have you heard the stories of Moses parting the Red Sea, Jonah being swallowed by the big fish, or Jesus being born in Bethlehem? Are these all elaborately concocted fables? Have scholars and pastors kept the ploy alive for religious purposes or just to keep their jobs? Does God really exist?

From your background and experience, you've already formed an opinion on God's presence and nature. You've pieced together comments from significant people and insights from your observation of life and made some determination about God. So what's your take?

See if your *God-perspective* falls into one of these groups.

> **I am God.** Maybe this is a bit over the top, but it's certainly an option. You may think you're at the center of the universe and in control of all that happens. If that's your take, you're in for a big shock. Unless you're like Jim Carrey's character in the movie, *Bruce Almighty,* where God gives Carrey's character the ability to be God for a short time, you'll soon realize there is very little you can control. Sorry to disappoint you, but you're not God.

> **There is no God.** If you claim this, you're called an atheist. *Theos* is the Greek word for God. The prefix *a* negates a thought, so an *a* plus *theist* is a person who disregards the concept of any god, believing instead that everything has occurred by accident and we're left on our own to handle the circumstance we find ourselves in.

The term *secular* also has an atheistic connotation. It means *separate* from God. A secular society is a community organized apart from the influence of God and His truth. Modern day America may not be overflowing with pure atheism, but it's largely a secular society. It no longer centers itself on the idea of a God, but continues to distance social values from theistic consideration.

> **There is a God.** Logically the term for this is a *theist*, a person who believes God exists. A pure theist also believes God interacts personally with His creation. The Bible says it like this:

"And without faith it is impossible to please God, because anyone who comes to him must believe that he exists and that he rewards those who earnestly seek him" (Hebrews 11:6).

There are variations to the theistic perspective. A *monotheist* believes in one God. A *polytheist* acknowledges many gods. A *pantheist* thinks God is in all things and therefore synonymous with the universe. A *deist* agrees a deity exists, but perceives God as impersonal and aloof from the world. So which one fits you?

My friend, Charlie, was raised by foster parents and always wondered who his birth father was. Was he tall and muscular? Was he talented in music or sports? Did he work as a fireman or a teacher? How far away did he live? Built into Charlie was a natural desire to find his father and hope he would someday have a loving relationship with him. Yet he never questioned whether his father existed. Charlie's own existence was enough logical proof that his father was out there.

Whatever you claim to be, there's an innate awareness in you that says you're more than a bag of DNA or a random blip on the screen of history. You were wired to look for your heavenly Father and to desire a relationship with Him. He is out there. In fact, He may be closer than you think.

Point to Ponder: You have already formulated an opinion about God. Your experience and knowledge has led you to a conclusion about whether He exists and what He is like.

Question to Consider: What kind of 'theist' would you call yourself?

"Science without religion is lame; religion without science is blind."
- Albert Einstein

Okay, Sherlock, pay attention. It's time to look for the clues. Does God exist? Pull out your magnifying glass and look closely at the universe. Romans 1:20 states, "For since the creation of the world God's invisible qualities—His eternal power and divine nature—have been clearly seen."

It would be natural to play crime scene investigator at this point and believe that science will reveal the information you need to prove or disprove the existence of God. But science has its limits. Many raise the objection that with the rise of scientific and technological advancement the notion of a supreme being is outdated and irrelevant to a modern society. Apparently we've replaced Jesus, who could heal disease, with sophisticated medical care found in our local hospital. And the awestruck biblical characters that witnessed God perform miracles obviously never sat through a *Star Wars* movie.

Would movie-going Americans yawn at the parting of the Red Sea? Has splitting the atom, landing on the moon, and cloning a lamb demonstrated that God is a thing of the past? Not at all. The human spirit still longs for affirmation and satisfaction of the soul. That is something science can't provide.

Science can only discover what God has put in place. The theory of relativity was not created by Einstein and then thrust into reality. It existed before Einstein, but now it has been revealed. Science with all of its miraculous breakthroughs will never prove or disprove the existence of God. Scientific fact will, however, confirm the presence of order, design, and intellect behind the creation of our world.

Rather than starting the investigation in a laboratory, it would be better to approach the topic from a courtroom. The judicial system bases its verdicts on having a preponderance of evidence. Though the jury did not witness the crime, they can learn the facts, see the evidence, and make an intelligent decision about what they believe happened. The more data there is, the more solid the verdict.

Skeptics assert that God is not there because He cannot be seen. Is the invisibility of God proof He doesn't exist? At first, this may seem to be a problem, but it doesn't take long to realize that many invisible things are accepted as reality. You can't use your sense of sight to find love. You cannot touch hope. Your own thoughts are very real, but they can't be demonstrated empirically. You can't smell a mathematical equation. You can't taste a moral value. These are all accepted as real, yet are invisible to empirical senses.

I believe President Bush exists even though I've never touched or talked to him. When I come home and find a warm dinner and a note on the counter, but no one in the house, I believe my wife was home earlier to prepare it for me. When I find my car window broken and my CD player gone, I believe a thief broke into my car. Just because someone cannot be seen, it doesn't disprove his or her existence. His or her presence always leaves an impression.

If you observe the universe using modern science or your own empirical senses, you'll see the fingerprints of God everywhere.

> **You'll see design.** The universe is a place of order and beauty. The rotation of the earth, the turning of the seasons, the stages of life, and the balance of nature all demonstrate a remarkable order to the cosmos. If the moon were not in the precise orbit it is, the gravitational change would not support life on planet Earth. If your toes were not connected to your feet, you would fall over. If the hierarchy of the food chain were not in place, nature would collapse. Woven into this world is a design that maintains itself and is strong evidence that there is someone of intellect and grace behind it all.

> **You'll find morality.** Yes, there's evil in the world, but evil is recognized only where there is an innate sense of moral right. Even in a culture of moral relativism where everyone is encouraged to determine right and wrong with his or her own conscience, there are absolute values to which the majority of civilization adheres. With little exception, people do not tolerate murder, adultery, or hatred and everyone despises emotional and physical abuse against themselves and their loved ones. There's definitely a built-in moral conscience in humanity. Is it the result of survival-driven humans? Or is it because humans were created in the image of a holy God?

> **You'll discover spiritual need.** Life is more than empirical. If this world provided all we needed, man would be satisfied. If you're hungry, there's food. If you're thirsty, there's water. If you need entertainment, there's cable. If you need accomplishment, there's work, sports, or education. But no one is permanently fulfilled by these. So why do we search for more? Because there's a void within each of us that cannot be filled with what this world provides. It's in your soul. You have a spiritual need.

The needs of the soul are deep within you. How is it that a particular combination of sounds can produce a symphony that brings the audience to its feet or that a melancholy melody can cause a love-torn romantic to cry? How does an artistic mixture of colors on a canvas stir a response inside the heart? Why do words on a page make the reader laugh, cry, reflect, or feel suspense?

The intangible existence of the soul is not a result of chance, but evidence that your Creator lives. You will not find the fulfillment of the soul in this world. You have spiritual needs because there's a God beyond the empirical world and He alone can touch your soul and fulfill all your spiritual needs.

Point to Ponder: The existence of intelligent design, universal morality, and the intangible needs of the soul are strong evidence for the existence of God.

Question to Consider: Which evidence that God exists is most convincing to you?

> "The probability of life originating from accident is comparable to the probability of the unabridged dictionary resulting from an explosion in a printing factory."
> *- Professor Edwin Carlston, biologist, Princeton University*

The first four words of the Bible are "In the beginning GOD." Notice scripture doesn't start with a persuasive argument for God's existence. The Word of God assumes the reality of God. If you were writing a book, you wouldn't spend several chapters trying to convince the reader you exist. The fact that you're the author would be sufficient. God thinks the same. He is the Creator and He doesn't try to prove anything. He knows He's there!

In the book of Exodus, Moses found himself mesmerized by a burning bush and confronted with the prospect of leading the people of Israel out of their captivity. He tried to warm up to the idea and to predict how the Israelites would respond. What were his credentials? By what authority would he attempt this mission? "Moses said to God, "Suppose I go to the Israelites and say to them, The God of your fathers has sent me to you,' and they ask me, "What is his name?" Then what shall I tell them?'" (Exodus 3:13).

Once again, there's no long philosophical argument for the existence of a supreme being; God presents a straightforward elementary assumption for all of scripture. "God said to Moses, 'I am who I am. This is what you are to say to the Israelites: "I AM has sent me to you"'" (Exodus 3:14). No line of reasoning, just a flat-out fact. I AM. I exist. I am here. Any questions?

If you don't want to make the assumption God exists, here are some propositions of truth to consider.

> **> The universe exists.** Unless you're completely crazy, you'll agree the universe exists. Look out the window to confirm its truth. Science and empirical data attest to the presence of the universe.

> **> The universe has not always existed.** Without having a degree in physics, you can still understand the second law of thermodynamics. Basically, it states that all things are perpetually expending energy and therefore the universe is

moving irreversibly toward a state of disorder. That's why you continually have to clean your house, mow your lawn, and wash your car! Seriously though, on a cosmic level that means the sun will eventually burn up and all energy resources will be depleted. The fact that we're still here proves the universe has not always existed. If it had, every bit of energy would have been consumed by now, so obviously, the universe had a beginning.

> Something caused the universe to exist. Every effect has a cause. You're here because your mother gave birth to you. Similarly, something or someone brought this world into being. Here are the two prevailing options for how it happened.

1. The big bang. Astronomer Edwin Hubble discovered in the 1920s the phenomena known as the red shift. Light from distant galaxies shifts to red on the spectrum, indicating the universe is expanding. If you play the concept in reverse, it implies that the entire universe was once in one spot—a single mathematical point from which all energy, time, and space emerged when it originally expanded. Many scientists call this the big bang. If this theory is true, then how do we explain the order, design, and beauty of the universe? From where did the sense of morality and the depth of the soul emerge? The big bang seems terribly inadequate to answer these questions. You'll learn more about the big bang theory in week five, "Why the Conflict…Science and the Bible?"

2. God created the universe. Due to the nature and size of the cosmos, the one who created it must be greater than the universe. The Bible states plainly, "In the beginning God created the heavens and the earth" (Genesis 1:1, NIV). This means God predates the universe and He is not subject to its laws as we are. The Bible supports that description of the Almighty.

> God is self-existent. "I AM" (Exodus 3:14, NIV). God lives outside of cause and effect. There is no cause for Him. He has always existed. That's what makes Him God.

> God is self-sufficient. "For He has no needs!" (Acts 17:25, NLT). You weren't created because God was lonely, bored, or in need of you. God was not attempting to meet a personal need in Himself. He is complete in His own supreme being.

> God is self-eternal. "You are God, without beginning or end" (Psalm 90:2, NLT). God lives outside of temporal boundaries. That's why He can offer eternal life to all who believe. He's greater than the time constraints in which we exist. He's both the beginning and the end; the Alpha and Omega.

The theory that a powerful deity created the world brings the most logical explanation to the issues of design, morality, and the soul. If an omnipotent, wise, and intelligent God created the natural universe, then we can understand why the world has beauty, music, balance, and order. If a holy God created humanity in His own image, then we know why there is a moral code programmed into our conscience. If a personal God desires a relationship with His creation, then we can recognize where the longing in the human soul originates and why nothing in this world will satisfy its yearning.

Which theory seems most plausible to you? Which do you want to be true? Are you the random result of a cosmic accident or are you a child in search of your heavenly Father?

Point to Ponder: A wise and intelligent Creator, who lives outside of our natural laws, is the best explanation for the origin and nature of the universe.

Question to Consider: Why would the Creator of the universe need to be greater than the universe?

WHAT'S IN YOUR WALLET?

"What we believe about God is the most important thing about us."
- A. W. Tozer

Most of us carry pictures of our loved ones in our wallets or purses. They're stored somewhere between our credit cards and driver's licenses, ready to be displayed whenever an opportunity arises. Proud grandparents show off cute baby pictures. A traveling businessman gazes at pictures of his wife and kids. Young couples in love long to be near their sweetheart in the photo. The pictures we carry are important because they represent the relationships and responsibilities in our lives.

All people carry a picture of God with them. Not a wallet-sized, glossy snapshot, but an impression in the mind and heart of who God is and what He looks like. Some people see Him as a warm, benevolent friend, while others view Him as an irrelevant religious concept. In either case, it's an image captured by personal experience.

Sometimes the pictures we carry are poor representations of the actual person. Most people agree their driver's license mug shot is not the best photo ever taken of them. Pictures that are fuzzy or out-of-date are not accurate depictions of a loved one and therefore inadequately portray the relationship they represent.

Many people bear an out-of-focus or inaccurate picture of God. It can result from transferring their earthly father's personality or behavior onto their heavenly Father. Religion can misrepresent God as being contained in ornate temples or church doctrines. Contemporary media often portrays God as boring, irrelevant, or even comical. The problem isn't in who God is; it's in the picture we carry of Him.

An atheist was asked to describe the God he didn't believe in. After a lengthy discourse depicting a cruel deity who lives on the other side of the universe and is impotent in the activities of this world, the questioner responded, "Well then, we do agree! I don't believe in that God either!"

Before you decide whether or not you believe in God, make sure you're talking about the gracious and powerful God described in the Bible.

Here are some common misconceptions of who God is.

> **Dear Old Dad.** Sometimes people perceive their heavenly Father as a cosmic-sized reproduction of their own dad. That's a good thing if their dad was strong, kind, and faithful to their family. But unfortunately, many children grow up without a dad's tender care and instruction. If they had a neglectful dad, they may assume God is distant. It's likely they'll struggle with the fact that God wants to have a relationship with them. They may find it difficult to trust anyone called father.

> **Cosmic 911.** The independence of the human spirit gives man a false sense of ability. Often life appears under control and God is forgotten or tucked away for a rainy day. But when things go awry, dependent children run to their heavenly Father. Unfortunately desperation doesn't always produce discipleship. God is always there when it hurts, but those who receive the healing don't always stick around to follow Him, reducing God to a cosmic paramedic.

> **The Force.** "Use the force, Luke!" The *Star Wars* force is similar to some Eastern religions. Life energy is divided into good and evil, equal in power, but subject to an eternal struggle for balance. This impersonal power is thought to permeate the universe, but offers neither a love relationship nor a salvation that is secure.

> **The Enforcer.** Watch out, God's going to zap you with a lightning bolt! This maker-of-laws cares only if you obey the rules. He's a killjoy policing the world and He'll get the last laugh. Such a picture leaves out the grace of God.

> **The Big Guy in the Sky—The Man Upstairs.** These are just two of the many clichés assigned to God that are ridiculously inadequate. Whether viewed as a sugar-daddy, a Santa Claus figure with a flowing white beard, or a distant king these caricatures never capture the awesome King of Kings and Lord of Lords God really is.

> **The Religious Icon.** Stained glass and church liturgy produce a cold and ecclesiastical portrait. Thought only to inhabit churches on Sunday mornings and seminaries during the week, God is limited to the concern of scholars and pastors. Institutionalized, sacred religion replaces a simple, personal relationship with our Savior.

> **Waldo.** Where's Waldo and where's God? For those seeking their Father, it can seem like they're hunting down a familiar face in the crowds of well-meaning religions and denominations. How do you find Him? Is He really in the picture?

Before you decide God doesn't exist, find out first who you are rejecting. The real God is the giver of eternal and abundant life. He freely gives all the love and joy you can handle. Take a careful look at Him.

Whatever you can comprehend about God will be revealed to you. There is no excuse for ignorance concerning the Father because He has made all the evidence available. His nature and existence can be observed in these primary ways.

1. Creation. Examining the beauty and intricacy of nature will disclose the wisdom and power of the One who brought it into being.

"The heavens declare the glory of God; the skies proclaim the work of his hands" (Psalm 19:1, NIV).

2. Scripture. The authoritative documentation of the Bible claims God exists and describes His character and nature.

"This is the message we have heard from him and declare to you..." (1 John 1:5, NIV).

3. Jesus. The Son of God lived on earth and spoke of His Father. His clear descriptions depict a personal and powerful God who desires a relationship with each of us. Even more, Jesus was the physical representation of God to the world.

"In the past God spoke to our forefathers through the prophets at many times and in various ways, but in these last days he has spoken to us by his Son" (Hebrews 1:1-2, NIV).

So, what's in your wallet? An old and distorted concept of God? Discard the misconceptions. It's time to update your picture.

Point to Ponder: Everyone carries a picture of God in their heart, but is it accurate? Creation, the Bible, and the life of Jesus present the best representation of who God actually is and what He is like.

Question to Consider: What's in your wallet? How would you describe the almighty heavenly Father?

"The Bible assumes as a self-evident fact that men can know
God with at least the same degree of immediacy as they know
any other person or thing."
- A. W. Tozer

God existed before anything else in the entire universe. He's always been and He always will be. He's eternal. He commands the universe with power, but has compassion and tenderness for the smallest creature. He's all that is good and right. He's exact in justice, yet full of mercy. He is King of all kings, yet still loving to His children. He's present everywhere and contains all wisdom. He's the Creator of heaven and earth.

We, on the other hand, are minor in comparison. We've been around for a relatively short time. We're limited in our knowledge and lack the power to control the world. We're dependent on others and often make mistakes. It's impossible for us to understand the complexity of the universe or the concept of infinity because we're bound by the limits of creation. We're a speck of dust in the grander scheme of the cosmos, but we do have the capacity to know God.

As you paint the portrait of God on your heart, you'll find you don't have enough canvas. He's completely unique and far greater than our comprehension. God has no limits or boundaries except those that would violate His own character. He's the Alpha and Omega, the beginning and the end. There's no one like Him.

If God were explainable, if He were finite like us, He would not be worthy of our worship or faith. He would not be God.

Trying to explain the character and attributes of God is like an ant attempting to comprehend the workings of a computer. Any description only scratches the surface. Yet God wants us to know Him, and so theologians have categorized the qualities of the eternal deity to build a framework for understanding.

Two kinds of attributes can be noted. First, there are the *non-transferable qualities*, which are possessed only by God. They are the characteristics that separate Him from all of His creation.

> God is self-sustaining. God needs nothing. Although He loves us, He doesn't need us. He exists apart from His creation and is complete within Himself.

"…from everlasting to everlasting you are God" (Psalm 90:2, NIV).

> God is all-powerful. There's nothing God cannot do. He spoke and the world came into being. He holds the keys to life and death. He is victorious over Satan. He's so powerful He restricts Himself from ever breaking His own moral code. He has the authority to save a soul or cast it into the lake of fire.

"I am God Almighty" (Genesis 17:1, NIV).

> God is present everywhere. God is not only in every place, He's there with you now! He's watching, caring, and available. You are never alone, because your heavenly Father will never leave you nor forsake you. Even if you walk through a valley of difficulty, He'll be with you.

"Where can I go from your Spirit? Where can I flee from your presence?" (Psalm 139:7, NIV).

> God knows it all. No one can fathom the extent of knowledge this universe contains except God. He knows everything immediately, simultaneously, exhaustively, and truly. He's infinitely intelligent and wise. Most important, He knows you better than anyone.

"Oh, what a wonderful God we have! How great are his riches and wisdom and knowledge!" (Romans 11:33, NLT).

> God is in control. Our Lord is a sovereign Lord. He is the supreme ruler of the universe. He's in control. We are like people on a huge ship; our activity doesn't change the direction of the vessel. Only God at the helm controls our destiny.

"And I saw a great white throne, and I saw the one who was sitting on it…" (Revelation 20:11, NLT).

There are also *transferable attributes* of God. These are characteristics He desires to share with you. They're either the result of being created in God's image or they're attained by allowing the Holy Spirit to develop them in your life. Here are just a few.

> **God is gracious.** God in His being has a perfect balance of character. He's both just and merciful. His grace abounds, but He never compromises His holiness. All of humankind deserves to be punished eternally, but because of God's grace, those who exercise faith in Jesus Christ will be lavished with mercy and grace.

"The LORD is merciful and gracious, slow to anger, and abounding in mercy" (Psalm 103:8, NKJV).

> **God is holy.** As light is the opposite of darkness, holiness is the opposite of sin. There's no sin in the eternal God. He is perfect and holy, set apart from all of creation and pure in His intentions and actions. Night and day the angels declare this attribute more than any other.

"'Holy, holy, holy is the LORD Almighty!'" (Isaiah 6:3, NIV).

> **God is love.** Love began in the heart of God and was demonstrated on the cross. Love is expressed to us every day through His blessings. Every good gift is from your Father who loves you.

"Dear friends, since God so loved us, we also ought to love one another" (1 John 4:11).

> **God is majestic.** Beauty originated in God. Splendor and majesty are His. There's nothing drab or plain about Him. Real worship adores His worth and His followers reflect His light and glory.

"Honor and majesty are before Him; strength and beauty are in His sanctuary" (Psalm 96:6, NKJV).

Crowning the list of God's qualities is that He never changes. His consistency means everything. He is and will remain the same forever. His love and goodness will always be there. His forgiveness and mercy will be new every morning. His holiness and justice will never fail. His sovereign power and immeasurable glory will always be present. He is and always will be God.

Point to Ponder: God is so big and majestic it is impossible to understand Him completely. If He were completely comprehensible, He would not be God. But He invites you to know Him and to discover who He is by studying His revealed attributes.

Question to Consider: Which attribute of God is the most fascinating to you?

"The fool says in his heart, 'There is no God.'"
- Psalm 14:1

My sister once asked me, "Do you believe in God?"

She couldn't have picked a more awkward time to ask. All the family was gathered together and every eye was now cast on me. The unusual inquiry caused the chatter in the room to dissipate into an uncomfortable silence.

My confirmation day flashed in my mind. I saw my thirteen-year-old self, receiving a certificate of compliance to the doctrines of the church. The cameras captured me in an angelic-looking robe. I remember how proud my parents were of this religious rite of passage, but to me it was just a social outlet to meet girls in our church. I never gave the teaching much serious thought.

As an adult with several years of college under my belt, I pondered the philosophical issue of the existence of God. Everyone I knew who claimed to believe in God had nothing to back up the claim. I asked 'God-believers' if they contained the knowledge of the universe and if they embodied all authority to make such an assertion.

They simply responded that they sincerely believed in their hearts. As a result, I discarded the thought that a supreme being existed in reality. Whatever God these people talked about was merely a fictitious character created by their need to believe. As for me, I was smarter than all of them.

Years later I was living in Alaska. Trying to repair a marriage on its last leg, my wife and I moved to a small village only a hundred miles from the Arctic Circle. Hoping a wilderness adventure would heal our relationship, we lived in a one-room cabin in the land of perpetual darkness—or light, depending on the season.

There was a small group of Christians also living in the village. My wife began attending their Bible studies and I ridiculed their materials. Each night I read the study books she was given by her new friends in order to debate and mock them. Eventually, however, a spiritual light went on inside of me. I discovered the authority that could maintain the truth of God's existence—the Bible. Tested for its accuracy like no other book of antiquities, this documented evidence had been preserved through the ages. It provided more authority than my sister, my folks, or any preacher. It's the Word of God. I could not escape the truth it declared. Not only did the scripture teach that God exists, but also that I was in desperate need of a Savior because of my sin.

On a sub-zero winter day, my wife attended a women's study that met in a neighboring cabin. She stayed late after the study to talk with a new Christian friend. The truth of the Bible and the love of a Christian woman led my wife to bow her head and ask Jesus to forgive her sin and enter her life. When she came home she went straight to bed, frightened to tell me what had happened. But before she fell asleep she prayed for me, her atheist husband.

The next day, while I was walking along the edge of an Alaskan forest on the banks of the Yukon River, a light went on inside my heart. The truth of God's existence, prayers of my wife, and the gracious kindness of the Christians overwhelmed me. I looked into the beautiful clear blue sky of the great North Country and knew God was there.

Believing the authority of the Bible caused me to believe in God, which led me to trust Jesus. No longer an atheist, I dedicated my life to following the God who is declared throughout the pages of the Old and New Testaments.

If you haven't yet been able to make the commitment to a personal and holy God, consider Pascal's Wager. Pascal assumed logic alone could not prove God's existence, and there were compelling arguments on both sides. Therefore, he proposed a wager.

If you choose to believe in God and He doesn't exist, you've lost nothing. If you decide against Him and He does exist, you've lost everything. Therefore, if you place your faith in God and He does exist, you've gained eternity and all the heavenly Father provides. It makes the most sense to bet on God!

You don't have to see to believe. Logic and reason weigh the evidence, but at some point, trust has to be exercised. Just like we believe oxygen is in the air even though we can't see or touch it, it takes conviction to follow Christ. Faith is a willful decision based on reasonable data.

The man nicknamed Doubting Thomas was the guy who refused to believe Jesus was resurrected from the dead when his friends, the disciples, reported what had happened on Easter morning. It wasn't until Jesus appeared to Thomas and stretched out His nail-pierced hands that the doubt evaporated and he believed. It took visible, physical evidence for Thomas to believe, and Jesus responded, "You believe because you have seen me. Blessed are those who haven't seen me and believe anyway" (John 20:29, NLT).

Do you believe in God? If you're convinced God is there, how do you establish a relationship with Him? Jesus answered that question when He said, "Let not your hearts be troubled. Believe in God; believe also in me" (John 14:1, ESV). Jesus is the way to the Father. As you continue in this book, allow your questions to flow. Keep asking. Keep searching. Exercise faith. Your Father is waiting around the corner for you.

Point to Ponder: If God doesn't exist and you believe in Him, you've risked nothing. But if God exists and you do not believe in Him, you've lost everything.

Question to Consider: What are the most compelling reasons to believe in the existence of God?

QUESTION 3>

This past week we've discussed the existence of God, examined evidence for God's existence, and made conclusions about His basic nature. We discovered that God is the creator of all things and that He's good and loving. In fact, His essential nature is love. God is affectionate and expresses His love through relationships. We see this in His relationship with us.

God didn't create us and say, "Adios, amigos!" He didn't invent the planet, set everything in motion, wish everyone good luck, and then exit the scene. Nor does He leave us to ourselves to figure out things on our own. One of the great truths of Christianity is that God, our heavenly Father, desires an intimate relationship with us as His children. He pursues, leads, directs, guides, protects, and teaches us. Most of all, He desires intimate involvement in our lives. This is the kind of behavior we would expect from a loving father.

I have four children, and I love each one of them. One way I express my love for them is by being involved in their lives. I interact with them regularly and make it a priority to know what's going on in their world. Communication is the foundation of my relationship with them. My children know me and how much I love them by what I communicate through words, actions, and touch.

Imagine a father who has never had any contact or communication with his children. He has never seen or spoken to any of them. He has never written them a letter, bought them a gift, tucked them into bed, told them a story, or done anything remotely connected to a typical loving father. Biologically this man is still the father of these children. However, if he began painting himself as a loving, nurturing, and caring father concerned about his children, wouldn't we all strongly object? A loving father communicates and is involved in the lives of his children.

If God wasn't involved in our lives and didn't reach out to communicate with us, we'd have no choice but to think He didn't love or care about us. Last week we learned just the opposite. God is a caring Father who loves us very much. 1 John 3:1 says, "How great is the love the Father has lavished on us, that we should be called the children of God! And that is what we are!" God loves us so much that we naturally expect Him to communicate with us and involve Himself in our lives. The Bible says that God communicates through His Word, His Spirit, and the giving of His Son.

The Bible is God's gift to us. It's the primary way He communicates and reveals Himself to us. We can learn a lot about the Bible from the Bible itself.

> 2 Timothy 3:16 says, "All scripture is God-breathed and is useful for teaching, rebuking, correcting, and training in righteousness." Scripture comes from the very breath of God and our heavenly Father uses Scripture to teach, guide, and correct us as His children.

> God's Word is essential to our lives. The Apostle Paul instructs us, "Let the word of Christ dwell in you richly..." (Colossians 3:16).

> Jesus quoted the Old Testament Scriptures saying, "Man does not live on bread alone but on every word that comes from the mouth of God" (Matthew 4:4).

> The Bible tells us the Word of God is powerful. Hebrews 4:12 says, "For the word of God is living and active. Sharper than any double-edged sword..."

If we believe God exists and that He is a good and loving heavenly Father, it makes sense that He would reveal Himself to us, communicate with us, and involve Himself in our lives. It's also easy to understand why His words are so powerful and life-changing. After all, He is God! How do we know the Bible is the accurate Word of God? Couldn't it have been altered significantly through the years? What if there are some major mistakes? How do we know we can trust the Bible? These are the crucial questions we'll examine this week. And the stakes are high!

Point to Ponder: If someone loves you, it just makes sense that they would want to communicate with you and be a part of your life. The Bible is one of the main ways that God has communicated His love for us.

Question to Consider: How else has God shown His love towards you and others?

How do we know the Bible is true and accurate? There's a lot riding on this question. Either this is the Word of God given to humankind or it's not. This book either contains God's instructions on how to know Him and live our lives or it doesn't. Is it the truth leading us to heaven or is it bogus directions detouring us into confusion?

There's a lot hanging in the balance. This is not a question to overlook. The stakes are high and it deserves investigation. Nothing less than thorough consideration is necessary for something that will alter the course of your life.

Many people doubt the authenticity, validity, and accuracy of the Bible. They raise the following doubts that are worthy of a closer look.

> If the Bible was passed down through oral tradition, how can I trust that the stories are pure, accurate, and unchanged?

> Aren't there a lot of mistakes and inconsistencies in the Bible? I don't want to follow a book whose authors can't even agree with one another.

> Doesn't the Bible include a lot of myths and crazy stories like someone getting swallowed by a big fish, Noah's ark, and Daniel in the lion's den?

> Without copy machines and printing presses, isn't it possible that the scribes who were copying the documents could have made a lot of mistakes during the hundreds of years the documents were copied?

> Since there are no original documents, how can I know the Bible is accurate?

> Couldn't people have made mistakes when they decided which books to put in the Bible and which books to exclude?

> If it was written thousands of years ago, how can it be relevant to me today?

> With all the different translations, how can I be sure the Bible is accurate?

> Aren't there lots of holy books? Why should the Bible be more important than the others?

These are all valid, important questions to address. Trusting in the Bible as the guide to living and the basis of your relationship with God is no small thing. In light of these concerns, how do we determine the accuracy and reliability of the Bible? The best way is to proceed with the same type of investigation used with any historical book or document. Here are some ways all ancient documents are validated.

> **Manuscript Evidence.** This is the tangible evidence of the manuscripts themselves. A variety of information is examined in determining the reliability of manuscript evidence. Experts look at the number of manuscripts in existence, whether these manuscripts agree with one another, and the length of time between the earliest manuscripts and the writing of the original manuscript.

> **Scientific or Archaeological Evidence.** The validity of the Bible is also examined through archaeological evidence. Since the Bible is a historical book, it lists thousands of specific geographic sites, people, dates, cities, nations, and cultures. Did these places exist or not? Is the Bible accurate at this level of detail? Archaeology helps us answer these questions.

> **Historical Evidence.** The Bible is a historical book. It makes many claims and discusses many historical events, places, and people in great detail. A study of history is another way to examine the biblical record as either valid or invalid.

> **Internal Consistency.** The Bible is a collection of sixty-six books written by about forty different authors over fifteen hundred years. Do these authors agree with one another and show internal consistency or is the Bible filled with contradictions in the telling of one story by different authors? A close study can prove or disprove the claims of the Bible.

> **Anecdotal Evidence.** The Bible claims to have the power to change lives. That's a mighty claim that can be either proven or discredited. While this is a different type of evidence, it's often the most powerful kind that a person can encounter in their study of the Bible and the claims of Christianity.

Over the next few days, we'll look at each of these areas more specifically as they relate to the Bible. Approach each day with an open mind and remember the stakes are high when a person is deciding to accept or reject the Bible as the Word of God. If you want more information about any of the topics covered, there's a recommended resources list at the back of this book. There is far more detailed information available than we have time to cover in this daily devotional.

Point to Ponder: The Bible is a historical book with a rich array of evidence from archeology, science, and history to validate its authenticity and accuracy. To accept the Bible as truth is not a blind leap into the intellectual abyss.

Question to Consider: What type of evidence has been the strongest for you as you consider the validity of the Bible?

An honest skeptic of Christianity would say: "Since we have none of the original biblical documents, how do we know that the manuscripts we do have are accurate? The versions we have were written much later than the originals; we're reading copies of copies. It seems probable that the scribes could have multiplied and passed down mistakes during the copying process."

The crux of this argument is that the Bible is obviously a very old document and must have been corrupted over time. Experts address this concern by studying the manuscripts themselves. A manuscript is a piece or portion of a whole document or book. The same type of rigorous study that is applied to all historical documents can be applied to biblical documents as well.

There are two main areas researchers tackle to answer these concerns.

1. The Quantity of Manuscripts. Are there enough copies available to put together the whole?

2. The Date of the Earliest Manuscript. What is the time span between the earliest document available and the date of the original document?

The Quantity of Manuscripts

The question seems simple enough. Are there enough manuscript copies available to compare to each other in order to trust the accuracy of the document? Let's give this a more modern example. How does an expert determine the authenticity of a baseball signed by Babe Ruth? The expert rigorously compares the ball and its signature with other balls signed by Babe Ruth. The more baseballs Babe Ruth signed, the easier it is to either authenticate the ball or to identify it as a fake.

While this illustration is overly simplistic, the process for authenticating historical documents is similar. The more copies of a manuscript that are available, the more weight is given to the authenticity of a single one.

The manuscript evidence for the New Testament is overwhelming. There are more than 5,600 ancient manuscripts of the Greek New Testament, 10,000 Latin manuscripts, and

9,300 other early New Testament manuscripts—more than 25,000 documents in all! Prior to the discovery of the Dead Sea Scrolls, there was not nearly as much manuscript evidence for the Old Testament. When the Dead Sea Scrolls were unearthed in 1947, more than one hundred thousand fragments were found preserved in clay jars. These were pieced together resulting in eight hundred Old Testament manuscripts.

The obvious question then becomes: "Is this a sufficient number of manuscripts to determine the validity of the biblical documents?" The best way to answer that question is to compare the quantity of biblical documents with the quantity of other historical documents that are commonly accepted by most historians.

Other than biblical manuscripts, more manuscripts exist of Homer's *Iliad*, written in 850 BC, than any other ancient writer. They total 643 manuscripts. There are just ten manuscripts of Caesar's *Gallic Wars*, seven of Plato's writings, and only five of Aristotle's. Wait! What were those biblical numbers again? Weren't they in the thousands? That's an amazing amount of evidence!

The Date of the Manuscripts
Another important consideration in manuscript evidence is the date of the earliest manuscripts and the amount of time that elapsed between them and the originals. Most of the New Testament was written between AD 47 and 70. The earliest manuscripts discovered are the John Rylands Fragment of the Gospel of John dated AD 117-138, the Bodmer Papyri dated AD 175-225, and the Beatty Papyri dated AD 250. Many of the earliest New Testament documents were transcribed less than two hundred years after the originals and some parts are within fifty years.

The Old Testament has a different history. The Jewish people had such reverence for the Bible that they would routinely destroy old, worn-out, or tattered copies and keep only those in excellent condition. Consequently, there are not many older manuscripts. Prior to the discovery of the Dead Sea Scrolls, the oldest complete copy of the Old Testament, known as the Masoretic Text, was written around AD 900. Since the Old Testament was complete by 400 BC, with some parts earlier than that, there was a gap of thirteen hundred or more years.

But the Dead Sea Scrolls changed all that. These manuscripts, which included parts of every Old Testament book except Esther, and a complete book of Isaiah, were copied down by the Qumran community, which existed from around 150 BC to AD 70. This closed the gap by one thousand years. The scrolls also showed the phenomenal accuracy of the Old Testament and the meticulous care with which the scribes copied and counted the texts.

So how does a gap of one hundred to two hundred years for the New Testament and four hundred to fourteen hundred years for the Old Testament stand up to other ancient writings? Comparing the same books we looked at previously, the earliest available copies of Homer show up 400 years after the original and the earliest manuscript of Plato is 1,300 years after the original. Aristotle's earliest manuscript is 1,400 years later than the original, and around 950 years elapsed between the original and the earliest manuscripts of Caesar's *Gallic Wars*. The Old Testament stacks up well when compared with other books considered historically accurate by experts. The manuscript dates of the New Testament are far closer to the originals than those of the other works.

There are many other areas of study related to establishing the authenticity of manuscripts. I'm confident that further study of the manuscript evidence will lead anyone toward accepting scripture as truth. For further study, consider reading any of the books on the recommended reading list at the end of this book.

Point to Ponder: There are over twenty-five thousand ancient manuscripts of the New Testament carefully copied over several hundred years with amazing consistency between all the copies. God wanted to give us a solid foundation for placing our trust in His Word.

Question to Consider: How does the discovery of the Dead Sea Scrolls (discussed in today's reading) impact your trust or confidence in the accuracy of the Bible?

AARIS THE GREAT: THE ARCHAEOLOGICAL AND HISTORICAL EVIDENCE 17>

What if you and I decided to sit down over lattes and hammer out more than two thousand years of ancient history? Wouldn't it be fun to make up detailed accounts of kings and kingdoms, wars and revolutions, geographic details of cities and countries, economic and currency particulars, social customs, pagan gods, and religious activity? Well, I can't speak for you, but I'd have fun! I can imagine a great queen named Aaris who ruled the empire of Thoran and the Thoranian people. Throw in some subplots and a conspiracy or two and it would be a great story. We might even get published and find our epic tale in the fiction section at the bookstore.

But if we claimed our story was a historically accurate collection of writings from people who really lived during those times, the outcome would be different. People would chuckle and historians would refute our claim. Archaeologists could easily prove the great empire of Thoran never existed, and that the venerable Queen Aaris is just a figment of our imagination. We could kiss our big book deal goodbye. We might enjoy a short-lived stint on the talk show circuit, but only at the price of the respect we might have gained if only we'd been truthful.

Unlike our fictional account, the Bible **is** a historical book. Forty authors living during a span of 2,000 to 3,500 years ago wrote it. They recorded thousands of significant and plain-old ordinary details concerning the political, social, economic, religious, military, and cultural activities of their day. Are these details historically accurate? Is there any evidence to support the details found in the Bible?

Archaeology has helped show the amazing accuracy of the cultural accounts found in the Bible. In earlier centuries, Bible critics dismissed biblical accounts as superstitious or mythological stories with descriptions of civilizations that never existed. By the middle of the twentieth century, however, the ever-expanding wealth of archaeological evidence brought about increasing support for the historical accuracy of the Bible.

Certainly not everything mentioned in the Bible has been found and verified through archaeology. But interestingly, no archaeological findings discredit the Bible. In fact, on numerous occasions an apparent discrepancy between the biblical and the archaeological record was later resolved when further archaeological findings backed up the biblical account. The following are examples of just a few of these discoveries.

> In the early days of archaeological findings, there was increasing doubt that Moses wrote the first five books of the Old Testament. At the time, there was no archaeological evidence that any form of writing existed when Moses was alive in 1400 BC. Then in 1975, the Elba Tablets were discovered in northern Syria. These tablets consisted of twenty thousand written records dating back to one thousand years *before* Moses lived.

> For a number of years, historians named the existence of the Hittites as an obvious blunder in the Bible. Extensive archaeological excavations in the Middle East had never rendered evidence of a Hittite nation. Later excavations did, however, unearth the Hittite capitol and hundreds of references to the Hittite people.

> All the Babylonian records found during extensive archaeological digs showed that Nabonidus was the last king of Babylon. This conflicted with Daniel's account in scripture that described Belshazzar as the final king of Babylon. This was regarded as an obvious error in the scriptural record until it was later discovered in a Babylonian chronicle that Nabonidus removed himself from ruling Babylon for a ten-year stint in Arabia. While he was gone, he left the kingdom in the hands of his son, Belshazzar. This all occurred at about the same time Daniel was exiled in Babylon.

> Luke, the noted historian who wrote the New Testament books of Luke and Acts, lists Lysanias as the tetrarch of Abilene during the time of John the Baptist (Luke 3:1). Historians regarded this as a mistake because the only known ruler named Lysanias was executed by Antony in 36 BC, years before the time of John the Baptist. Then a Greek inscription was found in the area of Abila, which records a dedication to Nymphaeus, "free man of Lysanias, the tetrarch," dated between AD 14-29—the same time period given by Luke.

Archaeology confirms the historical accuracy of the Bible. In the book, *God Wrote a Book,* archaeologist W.F. Albright of Johns Hopkins University says, "The excessive skepticism shown toward the Bible by important schools of the eighteenth and nineteenth centuries… has progressively been discredited. Discovery after discovery has established the accuracy of innumerable details, bringing increased recognition to the value of the Bible as a source of history."

Archaeology cannot prove the God of the Bible, but it can validate and substantiate the Bible itself as an accurate and important record of history. No longer can the Bible be written off as a book of myths and fictional stories without any basis in history. Any attempt by a writer to make up this level of historical detail would be recognized immediately as fiction. While Queen Aaris of the Thoranians may only live in my imagination and never make it to hardcover on a bookstore shelf, thankfully, the Bible has a true history and a shelf life determined by its maker, rather than its audience. Read it sometime. It's fascinating stuff.

Point to Ponder: The Bible reveals over two thousand years of recorded history. If the Bible were simply a fabricated tale, every intellectual discipline would be able to refute it without question. However, archaeology and other historical works have confirmed again and again the accuracy of the Bible.

Question to Consider: If you tried to make up two thousand years of history, how long do you think it would take for the scientific community to refute your writings?

Where did all the books of the Bible come from? Did they just appear or did they drop from the sky? Did a weary traveler find them hidden beneath a shade tree in a far-off land? Did a group of people randomly gather different writings, put them together and proclaim it to be the inspired Word of God?

There's a lot of confusion about how the Bible came into existence. Many people believe a committee came together and compiled a large number of ancient writings. That same committee then decided to designate some of the writings as the Word of God and to leave the others out of the Bible. Surely if a group of people randomly made these decisions, it's likely they made mistakes along the way. Maybe some books were included in error. Perhaps some God-inspired writings were overlooked and can now be found in other great religious books.

The Bible is a historical book. It didn't appear miraculously, nor was it simply found and assembled subjectively. Its sixty-six books were written over a period of 1,500 years by about forty different authors on three continents and in three different original languages. It's true that specific church councils were held to formally confirm the writings of the Bible. It's also important to note that for hundreds of years prior to these councils, the Jewish people accepted the Old Testament books as the inspired Word of God. The early Christian church also accepted the New Testament books for hundreds of years before the first council. The purpose of the councils was to sanction the books already established and widely accepted throughout history.

These church councils validated what we call the canon of scripture. Canon comes from the root word *reed*, originally a measurement tool. Eventually the meaning of the word *reed* came to mean a *standard*. So the canon of scripture is the *standard* of what was to be considered the inspired Word of God. The Old Testament canon was confirmed at the council of Jamnia in AD 90. Remember though, the Old Testament books of the law, the prophets, and the writings had been recognized and accepted by the Jewish people long before Christ came to earth.

The twenty-seven books of the New Testament were progressively circulated, collected, and recognized as Scripture throughout the first few hundred years of the church. They were then officially accepted as the New Testament canon at the council of Hippo in AD 393 and at the council of Carthage in 397 A.D. The councils used a precise and thorough investigative process before ultimately confirming each book of the canon. There were five specific criteria by which each book was measured.

1. Authorship. Did a widely accepted follower of God write it? Did the author hold great authority and respect from within the church community?

2. Confirmation. Was the author confirmed by God as a recognized prophet or leader? Was the author an apostle or an eyewitness to the ministry of Jesus and the early church?

3. Accuracy. Does the book tell the truth about God? Is its message consistent with other accepted books of the Bible?

4. Power. Does the book demonstrate the life-transforming power of God? How does this book impact the lives of its readers?

5. Acceptance. Has the book been widely accepted by the Jewish or Christian communities as being the authoritative Word of God? Was the book widely recognized as the Word of God as it circulated through the community of faith?

This is how the church community pulled together sixty-six books and recognized them as the authoritative Word of God. Each book underwent rigorous scrutiny. The inclusion of specific books into the canon of the Bible was neither accidental nor arbitrary. The uniqueness and power of the Bible is clear to anyone who has experienced its life-transforming message. The collected works of Scripture came together exactly as God directed, designed, and intended.

Point to Ponder: For a book to be recognized as inspired Scripture and be included in the Bible, it would have to be already considered the inspired Word of God by followers of God for hundreds of years. It also needed to go through many rigorous tests regarding authorship, accuracy, and many other qualities.

Question to Consider: Part of the credibility for the Bible comes from its ability to change lives. What are some of the ways the truths of the Bible have changed your life or the lives of others you may know?

Some people believe the Bible is full of errors and contradictions. They question how people can trust the reliability of a book when the authors seem to contradict each other. So we must ask ourselves, is the Bible full of conflicting facts and stories?

People sometimes view the Bible as contradictory when they read different details about the same story. Most often this happens when comparing the Gospels where four different writers record similar events in dissimilar ways. Why would that be?

Variation is always the norm when different people recall the same event. Each gospel writer had a unique perspective and intent for including particular events or details in his writings. If a family goes to counseling, for example, the counselor listens intently to every family member because each has a unique perspective on family events. They all have individual reasons for focusing on some details more than others.

Think about the characters in *The Wizard of Oz*. If you interviewed each of them about their journey down the yellow brick road, Dorothy would offer one perspective while the Scarecrow, Tin Man, and Cowardly Lion would each offer their own. The overall story would be similar, but we'd expect to find differences in each character's details. Let's take a look at a few examples from the Bible and find some logical explanations for the different details in the stories.

Often writers will include certain details that are not included in other accounts. For example, Luke includes the visit from the shepherds at the birth of Jesus and Matthew doesn't. Matthew writes about the visit from the wise men, but Luke doesn't mention it. This doesn't mean there is a contradiction in stories, it simply means each writer focused on different details of the same story. Mark and John don't discuss the birth of Jesus in their gospels at all but focus instead on His adult ministry.

Sometimes the gospel writers included details that appear to conflict with one another. But further research may provide a plausible explanation. For example, at the crucifixion of Jesus, Pilate had a sign written and attached to the cross above Jesus' head. According to Mark, the sign said, "The king of the Jews." John records the sign as reading, "Jesus of Nazareth, the king of the Jews." And in Matthew's gospel it reads, "This is Jesus the king of the Jews."

So what did it really say? It's possible each writer included only certain parts of what was written on the cross. Another possibility is found in John's Gospel, which tells us that the sign was written in Hebrew, Latin, and Greek. This could mean there was more than one inscription attached to the cross. In any case, the overall message of the sign comes through very clearly.

Occasionally the Bible contains differing accounts that are not as easy to explain. Matthew 27:5 reports that Judas had remorse for betraying Jesus and, "He went away and hanged himself." But in Acts 1:18, Luke tells us, "Judas bought a field; there he fell headlong, his body burst open and all his intestines spilled out." So which was it? Did Judas hang himself or did he have an untimely accident?

One possible explanation is both events occurred. It's possible Judas hung himself and after several days his corroding body, scavenged by birds and animals, fell headlong and his intestines spilled out. This is a good explanation for how the body could burst open through the act of falling.

There are many examples like the ones listed above that appear contradictory. Most, however, are a result of the writers' individual personalities and the details each chose to include. Obviously and thankfully the scribes never tried to artificially unify every detail of Scripture. This is a demonstration of their respect for the Word of God and lends greater credibility to the trustworthiness of the biblical documents.

God chose to put His words into the hearts and minds of the biblical writers rather than writing them down on physical tablets. In doing so, He allows the personality, unique perspectives, and purposes of the biblical writers to come through in their writings. The end result is the inspired Word of God, uniquely expressed through each book of the Bible. Overall, there is incredible unity and agreement among the writings included in the Old and New Testaments.

Point to Ponder: God gave us His message through human writers. The books of the Bible reflect the perspectives, purposes, and the heart of each individual writer. So the text of the Bible is rich and full of character and diversity, but it is all ultimately inspired by God. It is the message that God intended for us to receive.

Question to Consider: Think about the illustration of Dorothy's traveling companions writing about their journey down the yellow brick road. How does this help you understand some of the different perspectives that we find written in the gospels and other parts of scripture?

DOES IT WORK?
THE ANECDOTAL EVIDENCE

20>

What kind of advertising works best on you? Is it seeing it on television? Hearing it on the radio? Reading it in the newspaper? Most of us probably put more weight and trust in what our friends and family have experienced than in any formal or persuasive type of advertising. We tend to put trust in products or companies that have proven worthwhile and effective for people we know personally.

This applies to other life experiences as well. If you're interested in losing weight, you'll likely seek the advice of someone you know who's done so successfully. If you're faced with a medical problem and you know someone else who overcame it, you'd probably go out of your way to discover which treatments worked for them.

When we see something that works for someone we know or trust, we'll usually view that experience as being valid, credible, and trustworthy. This is called experiential, anecdotal, or qualitative evidence. Experiential evidence is one more piece of the puzzle when looking at the reliability of the Bible. The bottom line is, does it work?

This week, we've looked at strong evidence supporting the trustworthiness and validity of the Bible. We've considered manuscript evidence, archaeological evidence, historical evidence, and internal consistency. But the most powerful evidence for the Bible is its ability to change a life, a family, a community, or a nation. In their book, *The Facts On Why You Can Believe the Bible*, John Ankerberg and John Weldon point out how the Bible and Christianity have influenced our culture and our world. Here are just a few of their examples.

> The founding and development of modern science and law

> The establishment of the first hospitals

> Modern education, including the establishment of many universities such as Princeton, Yale, Harvard, and Dartmouth

> The advancement of ethics by providing a logical basis through absolute values

> Protecting the dignity of marriage and family life, which greatly contributes to the stabilization of society

> Inspiring major contributions to the best in art, literature, music, and architecture

> Creating vast humanitarian endeavors globally

God's Word has had a significant impact on our culture and a life-changing effect on millions of individual lives. People who believe in Him have altered their view of the world, their treatment of others, and the way they conduct their daily lives. The Bible has dramatically transformed people's values, opinions, capacity to give, and level of compassion. The Word of God has an incredible effect on how people live out their relationships and respond to authority. In short, the Bible has been proven, over and over again, to cause positive change in people's lives.

A quick and unscientific survey was conducted asking people how the Bible has changed their lives. Let's take a look at a few of their responses.

"I know it's true because it works for me and it has consistently for years."

"The Bible says God comforts those who mourn. My mom died when I was seven months pregnant and God is the only explanation for how I got over that in such a healthy manner. I naturally pack away my emotions but through prayer, Bible reading, and God's love I managed my grief in a very healthy way and was able to achieve a balance between tears and comfort."

"The difference in our lives is the proof that His Word is true."

"Trusting God's Word has changed my life more than any other event."

"Doing my best to follow what God says in His Word has saved my marriage."

Thousands upon thousands of people throughout the centuries point to biblical teachings as having the greatest impact on their lives. The Apostle Paul wrote in the book of Romans, "Do not conform any longer to the pattern of this world but be transformed by the renewing of your mind" (Romans 12:2).

For more than a decade, I've tried to apply this passage to my daily life. Every day, despite worldly distractions, I attempt to renew and transform my mind by reading and meditating on God's Word. Each year I read through the New Testament and specific sections of the Old Testament to let the truth of God's Word sink deep into my life as the central guide to daily living. I can say with great honesty that the teachings of the Bible have been and continue to be the single greatest influence in shaping my life.

The Apostle Peter put it best when he said to Jesus, "Lord, to whom shall we go? You have the words of eternal life" (John 6:68). Each one of us has to decide personally if this statement is true or not. Anecdotal evidence is strong evidence, especially if you've seen a life changed. But don't take it from me or anyone else. There's plenty of evidence out there. Do some careful investigating on your own and see what you find.

Point to Ponder: The Bible is powerful and life changing. Every year more copies of the Bible are sold than any other book. The Bible has brought about significant changes in science, law, education, medical care, ethics, and the family. No other book can claim to have the same influence as the Bible. Most important, God can change the life of whoever reads its pages.

Question to Consider: What are some of the ways that you have seen the truths of the Bible influence our society?

THE BIG SPENDERS

by Jud Wilhite
with Bill Taaffe

It never occurred to Cheryl Riggins that she would accept Jesus Christ and then face the biggest crises of her life. After all, wasn't Jesus supposed to make one's life *better*?

Coming to faith was tough for her in the first place. She was from a totally nonreligious background. She thought Jesus was a fable figure and assumed that churchgoers were deluded. But once she did come to terms with Him and joined a church, wasn't life supposed to improve? What kind of God would start throwing her curveballs once she had submitted her life to Him?

O.K., God, I know you're real, she thought. *I've accepted Your only Son, Jesus Christ, as the Savior of my life.*

So now my family's going to go broke? Now I'm going to have thyroid cancer? Now the IRS is going to put its claws on my husband and me and take every cent we've got?

This is Cheryl's story, and what God taught her in the midst of adversity.

In 2001 Cheryl was making a handsome salary as the controller of a luxury restaurant. Her husband, Lance, was a partner in a highly successful architectural firm. They lived big—large, beautiful home in a gated community, three new cars, two classic cars, a second home. Anything they wanted—*boom!*—they'd put it on their credit cards.

Then came 9/11, and the restaurant began letting people go because of reports that Las Vegas might be the next target. Cheryl lost her job. By the following spring, Lance's architectural partnership had dissolved.

Lance and Cheryl had been living on credit for two full years and their family of five was more than $200,000 in the hole.

At this point they definitely weren't "church people." Their faith was simply in themselves. But Cheryl knew that many of her friends attended a large community church and that their husbands seemed unusually considerate of them. She herself wasn't a prize, but then again she had to admit that Lance wasn't a ten on the "nice meter" either. So she accepted an invite to a women's group at the church and decided to see what happened.

"I was a bitter, angry, foul-mouthed person, and I didn't care what anybody else thought," Cheryl says of herself at that time. "It was all about me—me and my mean spirit."

She wasn't expecting much. So when she was accepted by the church group—bad mood and all—she was a bit surprised. And within a few months, almost despite herself, she prayed a simple prayer, inviting this amazing new person, Jesus, to enter her heart. It was the last thing she thought she'd ever do—especially with Christians, a class of people she'd generally abhorred. It was a catharsis. She wound up bawling as she prayed.

Then, miracle of miracles, Lance and their oldest son, who were amazed at Cheryl's transformation, also gave themselves to Christ. A few months later, all three were baptized together, along with their son's best friend.

The Bible says that "in all things God works for the good of those who love him, who have been called according to his purpose" (Romans 8:28, NIV).

At this point, Cheryl's life was something of a paradox. She was alive spiritually as never before. But financially she and Lance were like the *Titanic* steaming toward the iceberg. Lance was a partner in an architectural firm that did not withhold taxes from the partners' paychecks. And for too long the Rigginses had neglected to set aside sufficient funds to cover their tax liabilities.

Fearing for the future and knowing that the IRS would eventually come visiting, Cheryl and Lance decided they had no choice but to sell their stunning home. And because they now believed in tithing, they wrote to the church a check for $20,000—one-tenth of their $200,000 profit—this from a couple that had never known about tithing until months before.

Cheryl and Lance now moved into the much smaller house they owned. She got a modest-paying job on the staff of the church. He hooked up with another architectural firm at a fraction of his former salary. It was quite a comedown—humiliating, actually. But God would take care of them, right?

Unfortunately, Cheryl and Lance's tax records were still jumbled together, stashed in a drawer—out of sight, if not out of mind. Cheryl, concerned for the future, decided to hire an accountant and get them in order. After all, as a baby Christian she had by now read the biblical admonition to pay unto Caesar the things that are Caesar's.

Coincidentally, the IRS came knocking early in the morning just one month later. Cheryl's dogs started barking. Cheryl rushed into the bedroom and woke Lance up. His first words to her in a low moan: "How many of 'em are out there?"

Only one agent was at the door, but there might as well have been twenty. The government is not polite when it comes to collecting back taxes.

"How on earth could we have been so stupid?" Cheryl recalls thinking. "To have the kind of money we did at that time and just to squander it…And to neglect doing the things we should have done with it, like paying off our taxes and all of our bills."

Within the next several days the IRS garnished Lance's wages, allowing him to take home just $300 a week. And the government decimated the family's bank and money market accounts.

There was good news and bad news in this sudden hurricane. The upside was that Cheryl's financial house was finally being put in order—a plus in the long run, even if done by the IRS. The downside was she'd have to sell her second house to pay the taxes. And where she, Lance, and their youngest son would live was anybody's guess.

Cheryl's paycheck at church covered exactly ten percent of their joint income. She noted that if she stopped tithing the whole check back to the church, they would have several hundred dollars more a week to live on.

"No," Lance said, "God has been faithful in helping us, so let's continue tithing."

For two and a half months the three of them lived on the $300 a week. It was a test of their newfound faith.

"I remember thinking that God is a loving God," Cheryl says. "His whole thing is trust in Me and I'll trust in you, honor Me and I'll honor you. So we decided to just trust Him to take care of us."

Cheryl and her husband put the house up for sale on a Wednesday in July in what was an unusually slow market. On Thursday they got an offer for $5,000 above the asking price. On Friday they got another bid for the same amount from a Hispanic man—this is no joke—whose first name was Jesus.

A buyer named Jesus! Cheryl didn't know whether to laugh or cry. Jesus' offer seemed firmer, so they took it.

Now the question was where Cheryl, Lance, and their son would live. This was what she figured that faith-on-the-fly must be like.

It's not easy to rent a house for $1,200 a month when you're making only $1,200 a month and have miserable credit, not to mention IRS liens on your property. Yet that is what happened. The Rigginses put down the $1,200 on a house, having no idea where they would find the money for food, utilities, and everything else.

You know what happened?

Jesus unexpectedly paid for their old home ahead of time. And then Lance got a raise at work.

Several months later, Cheryl was diagnosed with a cancerous thyroid gland. *What next, Lord?* she thought. The thyroid was removed and she has been cancer-free since.

Not long ago she was sitting in her church office, reminiscing about her journey and what she now knows as well as her own name.

"I know that God is a loving God and that one of His things is 'trust in Me and I'll trust in you, honor Me and I'll honor you.'

I don't want to be presumptuous enough to say my faith is so strong it can't be rocked. I believe there are many aspects of your life in which some kind of tragedy can happen and it rocks your faith.

But I do have to say when it comes to our financial background, that I can really look and see God's hand in it. I can look and see God's hand in our spiritual life.

Oh, and something else. I can say that I expect God to answer me when I pray. Whether it be a yes or a no, I'll get an answer. I may have to wait for that answer for a certain length of time. And I may not hear Him the first time He tells me because it's not the answer I want to hear. But I know I'll get an answer."

QUESTION 4>

WHY IS THE WORLD SO MESSED UP?

WHY IS THERE EVIL IN THE WORLD? **21>**

When God created the universe, evil wasn't in the blueprint. In fact, after creating everything, including human beings, "God saw all that he had made, and it was very good" (Genesis 1:31).

However, we can't deny that evil is really present in the world today. Just ask Mary whose eight-year-old son was wounded in a drive-by shooting. Or Susan, whose family racked up thousands of dollars in medical bills and lost their home when her husband became crippled. Or Steve, who lost the use of his arms when his vehicle was struck by a drunk driver. Every evening, newscasts bring stories of crime, cruelty, and wars right into our living room. Many of us have also suffered sickness, injustice, pain, or grief, and it causes us to wonder if God is really there for us. If God is perfect and loving and all-powerful, how could He allow this to happen?

The Bible tells us that our suffering and troubles, including death, are caused by sin. And "sin entered the world through one man" (Romans 5:12). That man was Adam. When Adam and Eve sinned in the Garden of Eden, "death came to all." But we still might ask, Why didn't God keep sin from coming into the world and polluting everything in the first place?

This is a tough question. Certainly, God could have created a world in which sin was impossible. But that would have changed a lot of other things too. When you think about it, the only way God could allow us to experience love, which is the greatest value in the universe, is if He also gave us free will so that we could choose not to love as well. Love must involve a choice, or it is not really love at all. When God gave us the choice to love Him and to love others, He opened up the possibility that some may choose not to love, and live their lives selfishly bringing harm to others. If we look around the world today we can see the pain that has come as a result of that choice. Many people have abused their freedom of choice by hurting others, and that's where most of the world's suffering has come from.

In other words, God is not the cause of evil or its creator. But in creating people with free will, God created creatures that are capable of good or evil. He is not to blame if people have chosen to do evil rather than good. If we have the option of choosing love, we can also choose hate.

If evil is caused by people's free choice, what is God's attitude toward suffering people? Does He turn His back on us? Does He say, "It's your own fault, now live with it"? No! God loves us! He hurts when we hurt. To give us hope He sent His Son, Jesus, to become a man and experience the full range of human suffering—including death. God not only identifies with our pain, He gives a great promise to His children who are going through difficult and painful circumstances. Romans 8:28 says, "We know that in all things God works for the good of those who love him, who have been called according to his purpose."

Point to Ponder: According to the Bible, the answer to the question of why evil exists is clear—but it's not an easy answer. It might be logically or philosophically adequate, but it's not emotionally satisfying. We still feel pain when we experience suffering or anger when we observe it. However, there is comfort in knowing that God is not immune to suffering either.

Question to Consider: Why do you think some people tend to blame God when they suffer?

WHY DOESN'T GOD PREVENT NATURAL DISASTERS?

22>

Earth has a history of catastrophic events. We have witnessed the devastation caused by floods, earthquakes, volcanic eruptions, tsunamis, hailstorms, blizzards, avalanches, tornadoes, hurricanes, sandstorms, landslides, droughts, wildfires, disease epidemics, and other widespread disasters.

Some natural disasters have human causes. For example, mismanagement of natural resources can contribute to droughts and landslides, carelessness can lead to huge wildfires, and unsanitary conditions can lead to epidemics. But what about disasters over which we have no control?

Natural disasters have a way of making us feel weak and overwhelmed. We're pretty small creatures, and if we get caught in the midst of such huge forces, we're going to get hurt. When disaster strikes on a large scale, the victims aren't even given names. They are just numbers, statistics. When we observe natural disasters, it looks like we don't matter much.

Jesus tells us, however, that God takes note when a single sparrow dies (Matthew 10:29). And God has even numbered the hairs of our head, so that He is aware when one falls out (Matthew 10:30). So how can we believe that God cares for us as individuals when so many people suffer and die because of natural disasters?

First of all, what goes on in the world of nature is connected to human sin in ways that we don't fully understand. The apostle Paul says that the whole creation needs to be "liberated from its bondage to decay" (Romans 8:18-22). When we human beings brought sin into the world, all of creation was marred. Our world was changed. Somehow, when Adam and Eve sinned, all of creation was affected. One day, in a new earth, there will be no more natural disasters.

Second, by reading about Jesus in the Gospels, we can get an idea of how God feels about those who suffer. Jesus healed the sick, restored the impaired, and comforted those in mourning.

If you are suffering from some disaster, you can pray to God and be certain that He will hear you. He feels your suffering and cares about you. You can also depend on His people, the church. They are God's hands and feet, and can lovingly help you in Jesus' name.

Point to Ponder: God cares for those who are suffering. People who have experienced God's love are motivated to show that love to others. If we want to communicate God's love to suffering people, our actions are much more effective than our words.

Question to Consider: What are some of the ways God has helped you when you have experienced pain or suffering? Who do you know that can use your help this week?

WHY DO GOOD PEOPLE SUFFER? **23>**

This is a reasonable question. We naturally experience a strong emotional reaction when we see or experience suffering in our world. When we see good people suffer we wonder, why did this happen to them? Where is the fairness? Where was God? We probably think about our own response towards pain and suffering and wonder why God doesn't seem to have the same response. Certainly we want to protect our loved ones from evil when we can, so why doesn't God always protect us?

If you think about it, you will begin to realize that this question is based on several unreasonable assumptions. One assumption is that God's purpose is to protect us from pain. Another assumption is that people exist who are so good that they deserve a pain-free life.

Some of the people who listened to Jesus made similar assumptions. They thought that human suffering was a consequence of sin. If a person was injured in an accident, they assumed that the person must have done something to deserve the pain.

In Luke 13:1-5, Jesus addresses this issue. He mentions two events as examples. The first was an atrocity. Pilate's soldiers had killed some people from Galilee as they were worshiping in the temple. Jesus asked whether these people were more sinful than other Galileans. The second event was an accident. A tower had fallen, killing eighteen men. Jesus asked whether these people were the worst sinners in Jerusalem. Jesus intended His hearers to answer "No" to both questions.

So what reason did Jesus give for these tragedies? He gave no reasons at all! Essentially Jesus is teaching the people that suffering is going to happen. Suffering comes to everyone regardless of whether they live a good life or not. In fact, Jesus promised in John 16:33, "In this world you will have trouble."

If God's purpose is to keep us from pain, then this is not a loving response. But what if that assumption is wrong? What if God has a different purpose for us? Luke 19:10 says that Jesus came to seek and save those who are lost. And Romans 3:23 says that all of us are sinners. Jesus didn't come to make people think that they were good enough to make it on their own. He came to help them see their need for salvation so that they would come to Him and be saved from their sin.

So maybe we need to ask a new question: "When suffering makes us realize we can't make it on our own, who will we turn to?" At that point, if we turn to Jesus, we'll find Him waiting with open arms.

Point to Ponder: It seems no one is immune to some amount of suffering, no matter how much we try to insulate ourselves from it. God promises to use our pain and suffering in this life as a benefit to others and to ourselves.

Question to Consider: How does the suffering of Jesus affect the way we think about our own suffering? How has God used your hurt or pain to produce good?

Have you ever thought of the similarities between Jesus and the comic-book hero Superman? Both existed somewhere else before they came to earth. Both came to earth as babies. Both grew up like regular people. Both had a "normal" identity. Both possessed the power to do amazing things. Both used their powers to help people.

There are some significant differences, however. In the comics, when people needed help, Clark Kent would sneak away to change, and Superman would appear to save the day. He would catch the bridge as it fell, keep the airliner from crashing, stand in front of flying bullets—to prevent the disaster or to fix everything afterwards.

Jesus wasn't that kind of superhero. He was always who He was. People knew what He looked like, where He came from, how He talked. When He did a miracle, He did it as Jesus. He didn't go somewhere to put on a costume. And He didn't always prevent disaster. Some sick people died before He got there, so He raised them from the dead. He let the storm rage for a while before stopping it. And most of His miracles involved helping people one-on-one. He didn't rid the world of leprosy; the only ones who were healed were the ones He touched. Though He healed many people, many others remained blind, lame, and demon possessed.

When disaster comes, many of us would like Jesus to act like a superhero who will fly in and dramatically fix everything for us. Jesus does not operate the same way that Superman does, but He is a lot more help than any comic-book superhero could ever be. All we need to do is call on Him, and He's there. He has promised never to abandon us in times of trouble. He usually doesn't choose to do away with the disaster and fix all our problems. But He's there to help us through whatever we experience.

If you're in the middle of a personal disaster, look around for evidence of God's presence. He's there in the hearts and hands of His people who care for the poor, the sick, and the suffering. He can encourage you, comfort you, advise you, meet your needs, and give you the strength to keep going. And when the disaster has passed, He's there to guide you and walk beside you for the rest of your life.

Point to Ponder: Suffering, evil, sickness, and death entered the world at the time of the fall of Adam and Eve in the Garden of Eden. The continued sin of humanity adds to the growing tide of evil and suffering in the world.

Question to Consider: Do you know someone who is suffering? What can you do today to show the love of God to that person?

HOW CAN I LIVE WITHOUT FEAR?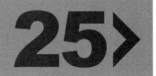

How does a young child conquer fear? Whether the child is afraid of roller skating, riding a bicycle, going down a slide, or stepping onto an escalator, the solution of choice is usually the same:

The child holds on to a parent's hand—then proceeds without fear.

Why does this work? As long as the child can feel the supporting hand of someone he or she loves and trusts, fear stays away. In fact, what was a fearful prospect just a few minutes earlier is often transformed into an adventure! Instead of crying and cowering in fear, the child is giggling in eager anticipation.

As we grow up, we're told that we no longer need this kind of support. We're big people. We should be able to handle problems on our own. So we put on a brave face, hide our fear, and stoically keep trudging forward. We want to look brave, even when we're quaking inside.

God doesn't expect us to live that way. Even though we face pain and suffering in this world, and we encounter things that cause anxiety or fear—God wants us to trust Him. God knows that we still need a hand to hold on to. God is with us letting us know that no matter what it may be, we can face that fear.

How can we look directly at our fear, realize its seriousness, and still find the strength to go on? The same way a child finds courage from a parent. Jesus said that if we bring our troubles and concerns to Him, He will give us rest (Matthew 11:29). The apostle Peter says we can cast all our anxieties on Him because He cares for us (1 Peter 5:7). The apostle John tells us that God is love (1 John 4:16) and that perfect love drives out fear (4:18).

When we cling to God, who loves us perfectly, our fear goes away. His love drives out fear—just as a child's fear disappears when holding a loving parent's hand.

Point to Ponder: We have a strong desire to know that God will be there for us in our own time of fear or anxiety. God was very clear on this matter. He said, "Never will I leave you; never will I forsake you" (Hebrews 13:5).

Question to Consider: Think about when you were going through a fearful time. In what ways were you able to sense the presence of God? Take some time to thank Him for His presence with you.

When we face pain and hardship in our life it causes us to ask some hard questions. Does God see what is happening to me? Does God care about what I am going through? Is God on my side? The Psalmist wrestled with these questions and cried out "My soul is in anguish. How long, O Lord, how long? Turn O Lord, and deliver me; save me because of your unfailing love" (Psalm 6:3-4). When you sift these tough questions down to their cores, they are really asking, God, do you love me? There is a longing to know that God not only sees what we are going through and cares, but that He truly loves us.

Love is a basic human need, and we never outgrow it. We were made to need other people and to be needed by others. As we grow from infant to toddler, to child, to adolescent, to adult we need to know that we are loved. When children grow up without such a sense of belonging, the consequences are tragic. Fortunately, God loves us completely; He meets this need in our life.

From the beginning of the Bible, God is pictured as a personal God. He talks with Adam and Eve in the Garden. He talks with Noah, Abraham, and many others. He establishes special relationships with people. He gives people laws that show people how to relate to Him and to each other. He saves them from difficulty, delivers them from slavery, does incredible deeds for them, and promises that He will never leave them.

But someone might say, "These are very nice stories, but they don't have a lot to do with me today. Those things happened thousands of years ago. God feels very distant from me today." How can I really know that God loves me?

The answer is Jesus. No one forced Jesus to become a human being and die for us. He did it out of love. The apostle John says, "This is how we know what love is: Jesus Christ laid down his life for us...We love because he first loved us" (1 John 3:16, 4:19).

Someone might still say, "That's still just a story. I can't see or feel the love of Jesus. So how do I know it really exists?" Again, John has an interesting insight: "No one has ever seen God; but if we love one another, God lives in us and his love is made complete in us" (1 John 4:12). We can't see God, but we can see His people. We can't feel Him, but the hands of His people can comfort and encourage us.

God loved us enough to send His Son to die for us. Then He sent the Holy Spirit to live in His people so that they could love us too. That's how we know God loves us.

Point to Ponder: Paul prayed that his readers would be able "to grasp how wide and long and high and deep is the love of Christ, and to know this love that surpasses knowledge" (Ephesians 3:18-19). This is a project that will take us a whole lifetime, and all eternity as well.

Question to Consider: What does God's love mean to you? How would you try to describe that love to someone else?

A DIFFERENT VIEW OF DEATH 27>

I can remember exactly where I was, and the feelings of sadness that washed over me when my brother called and told me that my father had a severe stroke and he wasn't expected to make it through the night. Many who are reading these words have received similar phone calls. In the realm of pain and suffering, death certainly ranks near the top. The loss of our life or the loss of someone we love is generally considered one of life's greatest experiences of pain and suffering.

Followers of Christ can experience the genuine sadness that usually accompanies the death of a loved one from a different viewpoint. They can also look at their own death from a completely different perspective. The apostle Paul wrote to some Christians who had experienced the death of a few of their friends. He told them that he does not want them to "grieve like the rest of men, who have no hope" (1 Thess. 4:13). Notice, he did not tell them not to grieve, but rather to grieve from the rich vantage point of hope. He instructed them to encourage one another with the truth that "we will be with the Lord forever"(1 Thess. 4:17). The promise of eternal life completely changes our view of death; it is not an ending but rather a beginning for a follower of Christ. This prompted the apostle Paul to write, "Death has been swallowed up in victory. Where, O death, is your victory? Where, O death, is your sting?" (1 Cor. 15:54b-55).

The truth of eternal life caused the apostle Paul to look at his own death as a gain. He wrote to the church in Philippi, "For me to live is Christ and to die is gain. If I am to go on living in the body, this will mean fruitful labor for me. Yet what shall I choose? I do not know! I am torn between the two: I desire to depart and be with Christ, which is better by far; but it is more necessary for you that I remain in the body" (Philippians 1:21-24). When we are following Christ and growing to love Him, we can also look forward to the day that we will get to be with Him forever. Our view of death can change. The Bible speaks of this internal desire to eventually come to our heavenly home. Second Corinthians 5:1-2 says, "Now we know that if the earthly tent we live in is destroyed, we have a building from God, an eternal house in heaven, not built by human hands. Meanwhile we groan, longing to be clothed with our heavenly dwelling."

The truth of eternal life will not only change our view of death, it will also help followers of Christ gain a different perspective about our suffering here on earth. The grandeur of heaven and a life spent with God forever can make the temporary nature of our sufferings on earth seem different to us. Paul wrote, "Therefore we do not lose heart. Though outwardly we are wasting away, yet inwardly we are being renewed day by day. For our light and momentary troubles are achieving for us an eternal glory that far outweighs them all. So we fix our eyes not on what is seen but on what is unseen. For what is seen is temporary, but what is unseen is eternal" (2 Cor. 4:16-18). Paul also wrote, "I consider that our present sufferings are not worth comparing with the glory that will be revealed in us" (Romans 8:18). So the apostle Paul, who experienced tremendous suffering in his life, helps us to see the pain and difficulty we experience here on earth from a different vantage point.

The Bible doesn't give us a lot of detail about what happens after we die, but it does give us two really important facts: (1) there is life after death, and (2) followers of Christ will go to a place of unspeakable joy and experience life with God that will last forever. Death is not the end. Jesus said, "I am going there [heaven] to prepare a place for you. And if I go and prepare a place for you, I will come back and take you to be with me that you also may be where I am" (John 14:2-3).

Point to Ponder: The relationship I have with Jesus now will last forever.

Question to Consider: How will an eternal perspective help me change my thoughts about life and suffering?

QUESTION 5>

WHY THE CONFLICT... SCIENCE AND THE BIBLE?

28>

Many people view science as fascinating and full of intrigue. We certainly benefit from scientific discovery every day. Just consider the progress in medical science. Forty years ago my father had heart surgery and was given a fifty-fifty chance of survival. Today, the same surgery is routine and performed every day, but back then it was rare and life-threatening. Imagine what advancements science might make in the medical field after another forty years. Maybe we'll be taking medicine that clears blocked arteries; one can only hope.

Many questions of faith and religion are not answered through scientific experiments. Some people say either you believe or you don't and that's what faith is. Others might have had a religious experience of some sort, like God speaking to them, so they feel compelled to believe. To many people outside of the church walls, faith is both blind and irrational. Here are just a few examples.

Mark Twain joked that faith is "believing what you know ain't so."[1] H.L. Mencken, the American anti-supernaturalist critic of Christianity, once said, "Faith may be defined briefly as an illogical belief in the occurrence of the improbable."[2] Evolutionary biologist, professor, and famous atheist Richard Dawkins said, "Faith is the great cop-out, the great excuse to evade the need to think and evaluate evidence. Faith is belief in spite of, even perhaps because of, the lack of evidence."[3] Christian author and professor Paul Little told a story of a Sunday school teacher who asked the class, "What is faith?" To this question a young boy quickly answered, "Believing something you know isn't true."[4] I wonder where he got that idea?

From the time of Jesus to the present, faith has never been unreasonable. The overarching issue as we begin this week is whether or not thinking people can embrace faith in an age of scientific discovery. We'll tackle questions like: "Has science made God obsolete? Are faith in God and scientific knowledge incompatible? Does knowledge from science outweigh religious knowledge? Which one is more reliable, and what do we do when they contradict one another?"

Compared to scientific discovery, religious claims in modern day culture are viewed with less credibility. In the realm of science, faith in God, the Bible, and Jesus Christ are seen as **personal-based** claims unlike the **knowledge-based** claims of science.

Christians have always understood there are two books: the book of nature and the book of revelation (The Bible). The book of nature is the observable universe with the discipline of science as her reader. The book of revelation is God's spoken truth to humanity. For Christians, both of these books have the same author and therefore should be integrated at some level. So the real question becomes: "Can science be done with God in mind?"

The modern-day gatekeepers of science emphatically say, "No!" They also say, "Sure you can believe in God, but in the real world, science is equated with knowledge and religion with faith. These two are not equal."

Science has become the owner of knowledge in society, accompanied by the modern philosophy of naturalism. This is the view that all life arose spontaneously from non-living matter and then evolved by purely naturalistic means. In other words, chance combined with physical law created life on this planet and evolved it to its present state. This idea is embodied by Carl Sagan's famous words: "The Cosmos is all that is or ever was or ever will be."[5] God is excluded. He's not required to explain anything having to do with the natural world. Scientific explanations are limited to natural processes and the laws of nature, so supernatural explanations cannot be offered to inform or augment science in any way.

However, both science and faith (theology) **DO** make knowledge claims. For example, Christian belief is founded on history and evidence. Arguments for God's existence can be offered as evidence for our knowledge of Him. The difference is that science and faith view reality through two different windows. The late Stephen Jay Gould, famous Harvard paleontologist and champion of Darwinian evolution, believed science and faith occupy distinctly different *magisteria,* or domains. He called this philosophy NOMA (non-overlapping magisteria). Gould said, "The net of science covers the empirical universe…[while] the net of religion extends over questions of moral meaning and value."[6] Galileo said, "Science tells you how the heavens go, and the Bible tells you how to go to heaven."[7] Are science and faith in conflict? We'll look at some of the details this week.

The issues relating to science and the Bible can be tough to understand and complicated, but don't give up. If you ask God, "Wisdom and knowledge will be given to you" (2 Chronicles 1:12). And God will bless your efforts to learn more about Him.

Point to Ponder: Religion and science are not considered equals in the field of knowledge. Science holds a superior position in western culture. Faith in God and the supernatural are not considered knowledge claims, only personal faith claims, therefore not testable.

Question to Consider: What evidence do you rely on to support your faith in God? Read Psalm 19 as you answer that question.

I remember the first time I saw the grandeur of the Pacific Ocean. The waves crashing against the shoreline in a seemingly endless crescendo were amazing to me. Awestruck by its power and majesty, I felt an immediate reverence knowing those waters could not be tamed by anyone but God. I marveled at the beauty and glory of God's creation.

What in nature leaves you speechless? Maybe it's the glory of a breathtaking sunset, the beauty of a morning sunrise, or the splendor of the heavens on a night when it looks like you could reach out and touch the stars. The psalmist expressed it this way:

> The heavens declare the glory of God; the skies proclaim the work of his hands. Day after day they pour forth speech; night after night they display knowledge. There is no speech or language where their voice is not heard. Their voice goes out into all the earth, their words to the ends of the world. In the heavens he has pitched a tent for the sun... (Psalm 19:1-4).

From its very first sentence, the Bible presents a Creator: "In the beginning God created the heavens and the earth" (Genesis 1:1). The universe had a beginning and God created it. The timeless one created time, and the limitless one created space. All time, space, matter, and being are the direct result of a willful decision by an infinitely intelligent being who set it all into motion.

The Bible does not attempt to explain how the universe was created as much as it says who created it. Because of this, the Bible doesn't limit its teaching about God as the Creator to the book of Genesis. All the biblical writers acknowledge God as the cause and Creator of all existence. Here are some examples.

David writes in Psalms, "By the word of the LORD were the heavens made, their starry host by the breath of his mouth...For he spoke, and it came to be; he commanded, and it stood firm" (Psalm 33:6, 9).

Speaking of Jesus, John writes, "Through him all things were made; without him nothing was made that has been made" (John 1:3).

Paul says to the Greeks living in Athens, "The God who made the world and everything in it is the Lord of heaven and earth and does not live in temples built by hands" (Acts 17:24).

The writer of Hebrews says, "By faith we understand that the universe was formed at God's command, so that what is seen was not made out of what was visible" (Hebrews 11:3).

Finally, Revelation 4:11 says, "You are worthy, our Lord and God, to receive glory and honor and power, for you created all things, and by your will they were created and have their being."

There are several things these passages and others imply about God and His creation.

> **God created all things "out of nothing."** There was no pre-existing matter that God somehow used to form the universe. He spoke and things were created. Paul writes, "For by him all things were created: things in heaven and on earth, visible and invisible, whether thrones or powers or rulers or authorities; all things were created by him and for him" (Colossians 1:16). This is unlike the pagan cultures and their creation stories. They always begin with pre-existing matter.

> **The universe hasn't always existed; it had a beginning.** It was created a finite time ago when God spoke all of nature into being. This doesn't mean God created everything all at once. At a minimum, God spoke systems of nature into existence. For example, He said, "'Let the land produce vegetation: seed-bearing plants and trees on the land that bear fruit with seed in it, according to their various kinds.' And it was so" (Genesis 1:11).

> **God is the author of life, specifically human life.** "The LORD God formed the man from the dust of the ground and breathed into his nostrils the breath of life, and the man became a living being" (Genesis 2:7). All the biblical writers acknowledge the historical reality of the first human couple, Adam and Eve (Mark 10:6, 1 Timothy 2:13).

> **God's purpose in creating the universe was to display His own glory and honor.** Isaiah speaks of God's sons and daughters as those, "…whom I created for my glory, whom I formed and made" (Isaiah 43:7). The evidence of God in creation demonstrates His great power. Jeremiah contrasted God's great power with that of the false idols of his day when he said, "Tell them this: 'These gods, who did not make the heavens and the earth, will perish from the earth and from

under the heavens.' But God made the earth by his power; he founded the world by his wisdom and stretched out the heavens by his understanding" (Jeremiah 10:11-12).

> **God delights in His creation.** He is pleased with the result of His work. He declares His creation good after each stage (Genesis 1:4, 10, 12, 18, 21, 25) culminating with, "God saw all that he had made, and it was very good. And there was evening, and there was morning—the sixth day" (Genesis 1:31).

The Bible is very clear about God and His creation. Spend some time today acknowledging His greatness and enjoying all that He made.

Point to Ponder: God, the creator and sustainer of the vast universe with all of its complexity, considers human beings the crowning achievement of all He has made. Your value to Him is infinitely greater than all of the grandeur of this world.

Question to Consider: Is God the crowning passion of your life?

THE BIG BANG: FRIEND OR FOE?

Genesis 1:1 states, "In the beginning God created the heavens and the earth". Today science says, "In the beginning, **bang**, there was the whole universe!" Is the big bang theory a friend or foe of Christianity? Do the Bible and science conflict on the most fundamental issue of all—the beginning of all things? These are reasonable questions—some you may be asking yourself or are being asked by someone else.

Yesterday we looked at what the Bible says about the God who created the universe and every living thing. The Bible teaches that God created the space-time universe in the distant past, and it hasn't always existed. For centuries, this view contradicted what people thought about the universe. As far back as Aristotle and through the beginning of the twentieth century, the majority of people believed that the universe was eternal—without beginning or end. Christians taught that the universe had a beginning; science taught that the universe was eternal.

Today the vast majority of scientists recognize, some reluctantly, that the universe began to exist a finite time ago. Prior to the 1920s science could deny the need for a creator or *banger* by appealing to an infinitely old universe. The universe, they said, was eternal; it had never not been! Why is it that scientifically this theory cannot be maintained any longer?

The Big Bang Theory
As mentioned in week two of this devotional, Edwin Hubble, an American astronomer, discovered in the 1920s that the universe is expanding. Galaxies are moving away from one another like dots on an expanding balloon. There are two implications to this theory.

1. The universe began some fifteen billion years ago and has continued to expand ever since.

2. The original configuration of the big bang was a state of concentration where all of the mass, energy, space, and time were contained in a single mathematical point with no dimensions.

These two features mean the universe sprang into existence from nothing a finite time ago. In other words, the universe had a beginning and was created out of nothing. Curiously this sounds just like, "In the beginning God created, [out of nothing] the heavens and the earth"

(Genesis 1:1). As the scientist, Robert Jastrow, puts it: "What is the ultimate solution to the origin of the universe? The answers provided by the astronomers are disconcerting and remarkable. Most remarkable of all is the fact that in science, as in the Bible, the world begins with an act of creation."[8]

Now you might consider the time frame of fifteen billion years ago and wonder if that contradicts Christianity. Some interpret the Genesis 1:5 term of a *day* as thousands of years, while others do not hold to a specific duration of time. Later in the week we'll consider time and how Genesis has been interpreted; but for now let us recognize the big bang theory as a friend of Christianity and not as a foe.

If the universe had a big bang, then it seems reasonable to ask who the *banger* was. The Billy Preston song, "Nothing From Nothing Leaves...Nothing," rings in one's ear. If nothing caused the universe and it just showed up from nothing, why is it here today? In response to this question the Christian answer seems reasonable: "In the beginning God created." The British physicist Paul Davies, though not a professing Christian, says the big bang is, "...the one place in the universe where there is room, even for the most hard-nosed materialist, to admit God."[9]

Not everyone agrees with this opinion of course. Stephen Hawking, a cosmologist from Cambridge University, said in a television interview with Shirley MacLaine, "We are such insignificant creatures on a minor planet of a very average star in the outer suburbs of one of a hundred thousand million galaxies. So it is difficult to believe in a God that would care about us or even notice our existence."

Before the big bang theory, science was able to deny the need for a creator by appealing to an infinite duration of time or an infinite universe. The big bang theory demonstrates that this can no longer be the case.

Robert Jastrow, director of NASA's Goddard Institute for Space Studies, said, "For the scientist who has lived by his faith in the power of reason, the story ends like a bad dream. He has scaled the mountains of ignorance; he is about to conquer the highest peak; as he pulls himself over the final rock, he is greeted by a band of theologians who have been sitting there for centuries."[10]

Philosopher William Lane Craig summed it up in this way: "Isn't it incredible that the big bang theory thus fits in with what the Christian theist has always believed: that in the beginning God created the universe? Now I put it to you, which makes more sense? That the theist is right or that the universe popped into being uncaused, out of nothing? I, at least, have no trouble assessing these alternatives!"[11]

The big bang theory, rather than doing away with a creator, has served to demonstrate that it's scientifically and philosophically more intelligent to believe that God created the universe a finite time ago—just as the Bible has always taught. The big bang is a friend of Christianity, not a foe.

Point to Ponder: The big bang theory is an example of the integration between science and faith and demonstrates that science should follow the evidence where it leads even if the truth points to a non-physical explanation: God.

Question to Consider: How has your understanding of the big bang theory given you more confidence in the Bible's teaching that God created the universe?

Every culture in the history of the world has held to a dominant creation myth. The term myth is not defined as something false, but as the dominant story or belief that brings meaning and understanding to a particular culture. Mythology in the ancient world provided a way of thinking. Creation myths were what ancient cultures believed about the origin of life and all existence. They have been found in Babylon, Canaan, Egypt, and many other locations.

The theory of evolution is a modern-day creation myth. In its various forms it has become the dominant view—particularly in the academic world. Most scientists view the theory of evolution as they would the theory of relativity or the theory of continental drift.[12] These theories are considered to have so much observable data and experimentation that they are accepted as facts of science.

What do you think most people would say about evolution? Is it fact or fiction? We learned yesterday that the big bang theory demonstrates it is scientifically and philosophically more intelligent to believe God created the cosmos a finite time ago than it is to believe the entire universe is the direct result of a purposeless, mindless process. Yet a popular high school biology textbook tells students, "Of course, there has never been any kind of plan to [evolution] because evolution works without either plan or purpose...It is important to keep this concept in mind: *Evolution is random and undirected*."[13]

It's All in the Definition
The confusion for most people lies in the way evolution is defined, or more often, not defined. We can think of evolution in two ways. First, *microevolution* is the idea of small changes or variations within species. For example, people grow taller, flies and mosquitoes become immune to insecticides, and animals adapt to varying conditions in order to survive. If they don't adapt, they don't survive. Nobody denies the reality of microevolution.

However, evolution as envisioned by Charles Darwin may be more accurately described as *macroevolution*. This is the idea that all species, including you, can be accounted for through small, gradual changes taking place over long periods of time without the intervention of God. The whole process is guided by natural selection—the concept of *survival of the fittest*, a completely random and blind process. The process began in some prebiotic soup where life arose from non-life and this first life has evolved into human beings.[14]

In summary, evolution can be defined as gradual change over time, moving from simple forms of life to the more complex, all the while being guided by blind processes as if by nothing but nature itself.

Three Challenges to Macroevolution

Having defined what Darwinian evolution is, what are the challenges the theory presents? Volumes have been written on all of the challenges. Below are just a few.

The first problem lies with the myth of prebiotic soup, often referred to as *abiogenesis* or life from non-life. How does life come from non-life? No one knows the answer—it's a mystery. Yet evolutionary theory requires it and an overwhelming majority of scientists accept it. The distinguished astronomer Sir Frederick Hoyle assessed the odds of life coming from non-life with an analogy: "What are the chances that a tornado might blow through a junkyard containing all the parts of a 747, accidentally assemble them into a plane, and leave it ready for take-off? The possibilities are so small…"[15] I can't speak for you, but I sure wouldn't board that plane!

The second major challenge concerns the fossil record. Evolutionists have been pointing to the fossil record as the factual evidence for evolution since the 1950s. Darwin himself wrote, "If it could be demonstrated that any complex organism existed which could not possibly have been formed by numerous, successive, slight modifications, my theory would absolutely break down."[16] Darwin predicted the fossil record would prove his theory. Has it?

According to evolution, the fossil record should uncover the slow gradual development of life found in the drawings of geological textbooks. Instead, the fossil record reveals what is known as the Cambrian explosion. There is no gradual development, but only complete development of animal life, fully formed and unchanged up to the present with no record of fossil ancestors prior to them.

Additionally, the fossil record does not present "numerous, slight modifications" or transitional forms between species. In other words, horses have always been horses, sheep have always been sheep, monkeys have always been monkeys, and humans have always been humans. The words of Genesis 1 make a lot of sense here. "And God said, 'Let the land produce living creatures *according to their kinds*: livestock, creatures that move along the ground, and wild animals, each *according to its kind*.' And it was so" (Genesis 1:24). The fossil record is not a record of the coming of life; it's a record of its departure and death as Genesis explains.

The third problem with the evolutionary theory is the complexity of living cells. Science has uncovered wonderful discoveries about the complexity of them. Bruce Alberts, President of the National Academy of Sciences, wrote, "We have always underestimated the cell... The entire cell can be viewed as a factory that contains an elaborate network of interlocking assembly lines, each of which is composed of a set of large protein machines."[17]

All these machines are composed of complicated moving parts. Take one part away and the machine won't function properly. They are undeniably complex. How did cells spontaneously develop to these levels of functioning complexities without an intelligent designer? Blind processes cannot account for these complexities.

Is Darwinian evolution an established fact of science? Consider the words of Cambridge anatomist Sir Arthur Keith: "Evolution is unproved and unprovable. We believe it only because the only alternative is special creation, and that is unthinkable."[18]

Point to Ponder: Evolution is the dominant creation myth of our time. Anyone who would challenge it is automatically considered uninformed at best. The most important point in any discussion about it is to establish just what the person discussing evolution means. How do they define it?

Question to Consider: How might you explain the difference between macro and microevolution to a friend?

Many people read the book of Genesis and assume because it explains creation that it's a book of science. But the Bible is not a book of science; it's God's revelation to His people beginning with ancient Israel in the Old Testament and finding completion in the New Testament with Jesus Christ. So how does a Christian interpret the Bible when questions of science arise?

I highly recommend you read the early chapters of Genesis, specifically chapters 1-3, the genealogical accounts in chapter 5, and chapter 11, verses 10-26, along with this devotional. Reading both texts will give you a background on issues relating to science and the Bible.

Why Genesis Isn't a Science Book

When reading any piece of literature, it's always important to know a little about the context, time frame, and the original audience. Genesis, chapters one and two, introduces two main subjects of the Bible—God the creator and humanity as His creation. It also sets the scene for the long story of their relationship. It's the opening of the Torah, the first five books of the Bible, which were written about the origins of the people of Israel.

These beginning books offer no scientific theories; rather they present the *who* of creation (God) more than the *what* (the actual process) of creation. Although they may inform science, they are not scientific. They are theological. The early chapters of Genesis also serve as an argument for the one true God of Israel over and against the pagan gods of Egypt, Mesopotamia, and the ancient Near East.

Genesis, chapter one, does away with many of the gods worshiped in Egypt and surrounding nations. Conrad Hyers explains, "On the first day the gods of light and darkness are dismissed. On the second day, the gods of sky and sea. On the third day, earth gods and gods of vegetation. On the fourth day, sun, moon, and star gods. The fifth and sixth days take away any associations with divinity from the animal kingdom."[19] With that as a background, how can we begin to understand Genesis, chapters one and two?

Author Paul Copan, in his book, *That's Just Your Interpretation*,[20] offers some interesting theories about interpreting the book of Genesis. He suggests our approach to these creation texts can either create barriers or open doors for a person on a spiritual journey.

We can be assured that Genesis is not a myth because it recounts history—an example of which is the portrayal of Adam and Eve as the first humans. This fact is reinforced in the New Testament when Jesus affirms Adam and Eve's historical existence (Mark 10:3-9). Other New Testament writers, including Paul and Luke, also acknowledge Adam as the first human created by God (1 Corinthians 15:45 and Luke 3:38). Paul even goes so far as to write about Eve being deceived by Satan (2 Corinthians 11:3). Jesus also affirms the historical account of Noah (Matthew 24:37), as does Peter (1 Peter 3:20; 2 Peter 2:5). At its core, Genesis points us to historical events, and yet it also contains a certain literary structure.

Genesis 1:1;2:4a has a historically poetic structure. Copan explains, "The prologue of Genesis (1:1;2:4a) is tightly packed and highly structured, using the symbolic numbers three, seven, and ten. Genesis 1:1 contains seven Hebrew words, and the first section of Genesis is divided into seven sections. Genesis 1:2 contains fourteen (twice seven) words. The two key words in Genesis 1:1 occur in Genesis 1:1;2:4a in multiples of seven: God (*elohim*) occurs thirty-five times, and earth/land (*eretz*) is found twenty-one times."[21]

There is an obvious tight-knit structure and economy of words that suggest the details of creation have been left out. The purpose of these early chapters is to summarize creation and present a great theological message, not a scientific one.

Another reason why Genesis isn't a science book is because the biblical writers regularly used observational language. They observed natural occurrences like the average weather reporter does when reporting the news. In other words, "The sun rose at 5:32 a.m., and the sun set at 4:59 p.m." Everyone knows the sun doesn't really rise and set, but to the unaided observer it appears to do so. This is the language of observation. It would be unreasonable to expect the observations of the biblical writers to be given from a detailed scientific framework, just as it would be to expect the local weather reporter to speak of the sun rising and setting in strictly scientific terms.

Because Genesis recounts history, has a specific literary structure, and uses observational language, we cannot read it as a scientific textbook. Rather, we must read it as a historical account that can inform science.

Point to Ponder: Leave room for understanding when discussing issues related to science and the interpretation of the Bible, specifically the early chapters of Genesis (1-11).

Question to Consider: Do you agree that one should read Genesis as poetic-history, rather than as a science textbook? Why or why not?

THE "DAYS" OF GENESIS   **33>**

Christians have a responsibility to understand the Bible. We should desire to know truth wherever it can be found. If we follow St. Augustine's advice then we have a duty to show that Scripture does not contradict what we have reason to believe from other reliable sources.[22] In other words, we must demonstrate that the early chapters of Genesis do not contradict known scientific truth. Yesterday we found that the purpose of these chapters is primarily theological and historical. So how do we reconcile them since the Bible offers no scientific theories or explanations?

In the text of Genesis 1-2, the word *day* is used sixteen times. Are these days literal twenty-four-hour days? Or are they longer periods? Apart from the overall debate with atheistic evolution, Christians have held varying views about the days of creation and the age of the universe. The three major explanations for the days of Genesis and age of creation are *young earth creationism*, *old earth creationism*, and *theistic evolution*.[23]

Young Earth Creationism

Young earth creationists believe the *days* of creation are six twenty-four-hour periods, just like we experience today. They also believe the age of the earth is anywhere from ten thousand to fifty thousand years old, and that the flood of Noah (Genesis 6-9) was universal because this type of flood can largely explain the world's geological structure. Young earth creationism was the overwhelming view of the church throughout the 1700s and remains a very popular view with Christians today.

The strength of this position is its straightforward approach to the text. Young earth creationists argue that the clearest and simplest understanding of *day* (Hebrew *yom*) means twenty-four hours. Old Testament scholar, Gordon Wenham, commented on the word *day* saying, "There can be little doubt that here *day* has its basic sense of a twenty-four-hour period. The mention of morning and evening, the enumeration of the days, and the divine rest on the seventh show that a week of divine activity is being described here."[24]

Others further argue that when the Hebrew word *yom* is used with a specific number, it is understood as a twenty-four-hour day.[25] The work of each successive day is also preceded by the statement, "And there was evening and there was morning." Therefore, any interpretation other than a twenty-four-hour period cannot be supported.

Some of the challenges to the young earth view include apparent discrepancies with modern science. Specifically, the evidence from science that indicates the earth and the universe are billions of years old. Light traveling from distant stars takes millions of years to arrive for human observation, considerably more time than the young earth view of the current universe's age.

Under this view, God would have had to create light with the appearance of age and at some level deceive the astronomer. Theologian John Feinberg explains, "As most of the universe is more than ten thousand light-years away, most of the events revealed by light coming from space would be fictional. Since the Bible tells us God cannot lie, I prefer to interpret nature so as to avoid having God give us fictitious information."[26]

Old Earth Creationism

Old earth creationists agree with young earth creationists that the Darwinian theory of evolution is false. They believe the universe was created supernaturally. Unlike the young earth viewpoint, however, the *days* of Genesis represent unspecified progressive periods of time, or the periods in between the actual days represent eons of time.

God then acted supernaturally between those long ages of time. They believe Adam and Eve were created recently, (fifty thousand years ago), but old earth creationists are divided over whether the flood of Noah was universal or localized.

The strength of this view is that it complements the findings of science better than the young earth view. Old earth proponents argue the word *day*, or *yom* in Hebrew, is used in various ways throughout the Old Testament and is not limited to a twenty-four-hour interpretation in Genesis. For example, Genesis 2:4 (ESV) reads, "These are the generations of the heavens and the earth when they were created, in the **day** that the LORD God made the earth and the heavens."[27] The Hebrew word *yom* cannot be understood as a twenty-four-hour period here, as this verse summarizes the entire creation week. Therefore, the days of Genesis along with the phrase *evening* and *morning* are literary devices used by the author.

Old earth creationists also argue that day six (Genesis 1:24-31; 2:19-22) is so active that it would be impossible for these events to occur in a twenty-four-hour period. Animal and human life are created, Adam names all the animals, and Eve is created from Adam's rib.

The question of when death entered the world separates young earth and old earth creationists. God told Adam that on the day he ate from the tree of the knowledge of good and evil he would surely die (Genesis 2:17). An old earth view requires animal death to occur long before the creation of humanity. The question to be solved is just what is meant by death in Genesis 2. With a young earth view, there is no problem whether death means physical or spiritual or both.

Theistic Evolution

Theistic evolution holds that Darwin's theory is true. Genesis explains the *who* and *why* of creation, but not the *how*. This is the job of science. Theistic evolution attempts the greatest integration with scientific theory by recognizing that God's method of creation was a gradual process observed in the fossil record of the earth.

As we learned earlier this week, evolutionary theory requires no intelligence in the process of nature. Theistic evolutionists reject the philosophy of evolutionary theory but embrace the science.

There are different variations to each of these views. Recognizing that there are diverse opinions within the Christian community, we need to leave room for disagreement and realize this is not as important as other topics. The fight is not over the days of Genesis or the age of the universe. As we will see tomorrow, the stakes are much higher.

Point to Ponder: The Bible declares the *who* of creation, not the *what*, that is, the details of how the world was made.

Question to Consider: Of the three views mentioned today, which one makes the most sense to you? Why or why not?

Regarding science and faith, Christians have not only challenged evolutionary theory, but are often challenging other Christians. The core of the debate focuses on the age of the universe and the *days* of creation. These are interesting questions but not the most important issue. All week we have sought to understand some of the questions and challenges surrounding science and faith. This process can often be confusing, raising more questions than are actually answered. We must realize we're all on a journey to understand very complex issues. The issue in today's study, however, is by far the most important.

The conflict between science and faith boils down to one's philosophy of science. It's really not a scientific issue at all. Rather it's the assumptions we bring to science. The gatekeepers of science have not allowed supernatural intelligence or God to be considered in the discussion. Richard Lewontin, professor of Genetics at Harvard University, expressed the following sentiment in an essay in the *New York Review of Books* in January 1997:

> The primary problem is not to provide the public with knowledge of how far it is to the nearest star and what genes are made of… Rather, the problem is to get them to reject irrational and supernatural explanations of the world, the demons that exist only in their imaginations, and to accept a social and intellectual apparatus, Science, as the only begetter of truth.[28]

If Lewontin is right, science is the gatekeeper of truth and belief in God is limited to personal belief. Darwin and his system of natural selection dismissed any reason for an intelligent cause of the universe. His theory became so popular because he got religion out of science. Christians need to shift the debate from questions about the age of the universe and the *days* of Genesis to *intelligent design* versus *blind watchmaker*.

What Is a Blind Watchmaker?

Evolutionary biologist and Oxford University professor Richard Dawkins wrote,

> Natural selection, the blind, unconscious, automatic process which Darwin discovered, and which we now know is the explanation for the existence and apparently purposeful form of all life, has no purpose in mind. It has no mind and no mind's eye. It does not plan for the future. It has no vision, no foresight, and no sight at all. If it can be said to play the role of watchmaker in nature, it is the *blind* watchmaker.[29]

What Is Intelligent Design?

The good news is there are some exciting developments in science. A new program of scientific research known as *intelligent design* is beginning to challenge the *blind watchmaker*. Some even think we could be on the verge of a worldview revolution in science equivalent to Galileo or Darwin.[30] Philosopher, mathematician, and leading *intelligent design* proponent William Dembski defines it this way: "Intelligent design is neither repackaged creationism nor religion masquerading as science. Intelligent design is a theory for making sense of intelligent causes."[31] In other words, intelligent design is purposeful; there's a meaning behind the complexity of biological cells.

Often Christians point to God for the answers to science without showing any evidence. Johannes Kepler, the father of modern-day astronomy, thought the craters on the moon were intelligently designed by moon dwellers.[32] He didn't show any evidence moon dwellers actually existed, and not surprisingly, science later proved that natural processes formed the craters.

So the challenge is to demonstrate that there is intelligent design in biological systems. In other words, can it be demonstrated scientifically that the complexity in any system (e.g., cells, DNA, or the human body) is there by actual design? Let's look at some evidence for intelligent design.

Evidence of Intelligent Design: The Anthropic Principle

The anthropic (Greek: *anthropos, human being*) principle states that the universe was fitted from the very first moment of its existence for the emergence of life in general and human life in particular.[33] This scientific principle points to an intelligent designer. Consider these examples.

1. The universe began to exist and bangs have *bangers*. As discussed earlier this week, the universe has not always existed but began to exist sometime in the past. Science refers to this as the big bang theory. This theory requires such precise conditions at the time of the big bang that even if they were just slightly different, no life of any kind would exist.

2. The universe is finely tuned. There are more than thirty constants of nature we cannot live without. If gravitational force was altered by 1 part in 1040 power, the sun would not exist and the moon would crash into the earth or blast off into space. A slight increase in the force of gravity would result in all the stars being much more massive than our sun, causing the sun to burn too rapidly to sustain life. If the rate of the universe's expansion were one-millionth slower, the temperature on earth would be 10,000 degrees Celsius or 18,032 degrees Fahrenheit.[34]

3. The incredible complexity of the universe. This refers to a system that is composed of several interacting parts, where the removal of any of the parts causes the system to cease functioning. This kind of complexity requires *intelligent design*. For more information on this subject, see Michael Behe's book, *Darwin's Black Box: The Biochemical Challenge to Evolution*, listed in the recommended resources at the back of this book.

4. The origin of the mind. Non-intelligence cannot produce intelligence and matter cannot produce mind. If you begin with a conscious being like God, then there is no problem accounting for the origin of the mind and consciousness.

These are just a few examples of creation that point to an intelligent designer. In the words of the Apostle Paul, "Now to the King eternal, immortal, invisible, the only God, be honor and glory for ever and ever. Amen" (1 Timothy 1:17).

As I mentioned at the beginning of the week, issues relating to science and the Bible are complex and can be tough to understand, but don't let that stop you from searching and finding the truth. Eternity is in the balance.

Point to Ponder: Intelligent design is not a special creation theory, but a working scientific model offered to rationally explain and detect intelligent causes in nature.

Question to Consider: What questions raised in this week's reading remain unanswered? Consider consulting one of the recommended resources on page 136.

THE LONG WAY HOME

by Jud Wilhite
with Bill Taaffe

Andrew Goldstein was a child of the '80s.

He moved from New York to Las Vegas as a teenager, graduating number one from Hebrew school, part of the community of some eighty thousand Jews in the city of the second chance. His dad worked at the famed Las Vegas Club, which allowed Andrew to hang around the likes of Kenny Rogers and Tony Orlando.

But then Andrew's family moved back East, pursuing a third chance, and he attended college in upstate New York. One part of him—the traditional Andrew—still pined for the B'nai B'rith Jewish youth movement in Vegas. It was where his friends and his faith were.

Another part of Andrew—the hedonistic one—grew his hair halfway down his back, pierced his ear five times, and got involved in weed, acid, mescaline, hash, opium, and mushrooms, not to mention booze. The hedonistic Andrew won. He still could chill out with music—always his first love—but he was blotto most of the time.

"It was like losing my mind," he says today. "I wasn't a bad person to anybody else. But certainly the Holy Spirit wasn't coming into *this* temple."

His parents finally took him home to Long Island.

He parked cars at a golf club, sold records in Grand Central Station, worked in a restaurant where he became pals with a then-unknown radio talker named Howard Stern, and dated the first non-Jewish girl of his life. Her name was Angela—a good Catholic girl who, when he unexpectedly kissed her on the lips shortly after they had met, surprised him by not telling him off. They fell madly in love, and for six years she put up with his boozing.

Andrew was funny—a scream on the surface, but serious down deep; brilliant in an unpredictable way, but also a wrestler with demons.

One day Angela up and said, "Andrew, it's me or the Jack Daniels."

You know what he did? He stopped drinking cold turkey. There was something absolute about him when he made up his mind.

He married her in a ceremony officiated by a rabbi and a priest, and in 1996 they moved back to Vegas, his favorite town. His quitting booze and drugs was either a God thing or he had summoned up power he never knew he had.

Andrew, now thirty-six, was running an Outback Steakhouse in a Vegas suburb, and finally was a partner in the chain. He always observed the Jewish holidays like Rosh Hashanah, Yom Kippur, and Passover, even conducting the Seder feast in Hebrew. Yet at the same time he wore a necklace Angela had given him with a Star of David superimposed on a cross.

Had you asked him about Jesus, he would have said that Christ was a historical figure. In fact, he always wondered why as a Jew he couldn't read the New Testament—unaware that it was written entirely by Jews, with the exception of Luke.

By 2004 Andrew's two sons were seven and five and he was making fine money at Outback. He had been attending a megachurch in the Las Vegas valley with Angela and the boys because he liked the contemporary and rock music they played. And, as a Jew, he found himself welcomed, not ostracized.

Once during a message the pastor asked everyone to close their eyes and bow their heads so that those who wanted to receive Christ into their lives could raise their hands and semi-privately do so. Andrew lifted his *index finger* so the pastor wouldn't see.

Now, out of the blue, he developed two potentially life-threatening health problems. He was told he had CMT, a relatively rare neurological disease that results in the gradual wasting of the muscles.

And worse, he was having trouble breathing while experiencing intense, crushing pains in his chest and left arm. Initial tests indicated a major blockage near his heart. Taken to a hospital for a test that would pinpoint the trouble, he found himself lying alone on a gurney before the procedure.

It was Andrew Goldstein's moment of truth with God as he knew Him.

"So now I'm lying there," Andrew recalls. "*Here goes nothing*, I say to myself. Everything I've heard churches say is going through my head: *Leave your troubles at His throne ... You're a sinner ... Here's your salvation ... Lake of fire ... God's right hand ...*

"I said, 'Lord, if I'm offending You right now, I apologize. I'm a Jewish man and it's difficult for me to ask this. But Jesus Christ, if You are real, I need You to come into my life right now. I need to know You're real. I need You to speak to me. Now, this minute. Not tomorrow. Not a week from tomorrow…

"I will submit my life to You. I will do everything I have heard. I will bow down. I don't want to die. And if I do die, I don't want to die not saved like this. I don't want to be afraid of dying. I don't want to go swimming in a lake of fire. I want to know where I'm going."

The issue for Andrew was the nature of the Godhead and his obedience to the revelation he was receiving. A student of the Pentateuch, he had always believed in Yahweh.

Immediately, Andrew says, God spoke to him, as if audibly.

"God told me I wasn't putting Him first in my life, as much as I thought I was. He told me that the deal I'd made with Him—*I'm going to work hard and be a good person and You watch my family*—isn't a deal He makes. And that my God was money—I'd put my job first. And He said, 'I'm first. I'm first above your family. Me—I come first.'

'Okay, Lord,' I said.

Then He specifically told me what I needed to read—first and foremost, Isaiah 53—very important that I read this.

'Yes, Lord,' I said. 'I'm there.'"

The conversation, such as it was, was interrupted by the technicians who rolled Andrew in for an angiogram, which shows where blood flow to the heart might be blocked. Twenty minutes later, they came back with the verdict. He had no blockage. But he did have cardiomyopathy, an irreversible weakening of the heart muscle.

This was the big one as far as Andrew was concerned. This was the number-one event. "Sometimes your children misbehave and sometimes the punishment has to be pretty huge so they'll learn their lesson," Andrew says. "At that moment I learned my lesson that I wasn't putting Him first."

Home again, he read Isaiah 53, which speaks of the suffering servant of humanity: "But he was pierced for our transgressions, he was crushed for our iniquities; the punishment that brought us peace was upon him, and by his wounds we are healed" (53:5).

He read Psalm 22:16: "Dogs have surrounded me; a band of evil men has encircled me, they have pierced my hands and my feet."

"This is my stuff, these are the Jewish scriptures," he thought. "We're talking about Christ! Are you kidding? Why didn't anybody tell me this? So that's why they didn't want us to read the Bible!"

Andrew Goldstein decided to make one appointment with the pastor of the church and another with his rabbi. He knew what he was thinking, but he wanted confirmation.

He met with the pastor for two and a half hours. He and his son, Zachary, already were serving as greeters just inside the church doors—two Goldsteins, it doesn't get more Jewish than that. What, he wanted to know, did the pastor make of Isaiah 53 and Psalm 22? Were the passages speaking of Christ?

Deep down, Andrew knew the answer. The scriptures were just so obvious. Andrew left with a growing awareness that he had become a completed Jew.

Then he visited his rabbi, who had a rebuttal for each of the Old Testament passages Andrew cited. But his explanations seemed rehearsed—in fact, they gave Andrew an odd sense of relief, for he obviously wasn't the first Jew to ask the rabbi these questions. Andrew felt a force field surrounding him.

"Who told you to read these things?" the rabbi asked at one point. "I think you're reading too much of the Bible. You need to step away from it."

Unlike some other rabbis, this cleric told Andrew that if he accepted Christ as his Lord and Savior, he wasn't a Jew anymore.

The decision was final.

Andrew Goldstein, Angela, his wife, and their two boys have been worshiping the Son of God, the Hebrew of Hebrews, in sickness and in health ever since.

QUESTION 6>

A widow sat with family and friends after her husband's funeral. With the painful knowledge that her husband had never accepted Christ, she cried profusely, "He was such a good and generous man. How could God refuse him entry into heaven?"

A bright, young student once asked his professor, "What about Gandhi? He was a good man. Doesn't God take that into account when granting admission to heaven?"

An intense cocktail party conversation revolves around a hotly debated question. "How can a loving God reject people who've never heard of Jesus?"

Have you ever pondered those kinds of questions? I've wrestled with them myself and at times I have even delved deeper with questions like these:

> > How do we know Jesus is who He says He is?

> > Doesn't sincerity count for something?

> > Did Jesus really rise from the dead?

> > Do all religions lead to God?

> > Isn't being a good person what God is looking for?

There's a bigger question behind all of these, and that is, "Is Jesus really the only way to God?" For many, there's no such thing as absolute truth. Truth to them is whether or not anyone believes something. They say, "There's truth for you, and truth for me," which leads to the belief that there are multiple pathways to God.

George Barna, cultural anthropologist, studies cultural trends in the lives of people. In 2004 he conducted a survey directed at adults who were not connected with Christianity in any way. The results revealed different perspectives regarding the *truths* about God. The results showed two main perspectives:

1. Only 51 percent of adults surveyed define God as the perfect, all-powerful, all-knowing Creator of the universe who continues to rule His creation today.

2. Only 23 percent of adults surveyed firmly believe that the Bible is totally accurate in all that it teaches.

Sadly, there's confusion even among Christians on this issue. In a recent study, 64 percent of American Christians surveyed agreed with the statement, "Muslims, Buddhists, Jews, and all other people pray to the same God, even though they use different names for their God." Sixty-one percent agreed with the statement, "If a person is generally good or does enough good things during their lifetime, he or she will earn a place in heaven." And 40 percent agreed that, "All good people, whether or not they consider Jesus Christ to be their Savior, will live in heaven after they die." Obviously, there's a common belief that there are many paths to God.

Is Jesus really the only way to God?
Jesus often made radical statements that contradicted the norm and caused people to stop in their tracks. He said things like, "The first will be last; rejoice in persecution; pray for your enemies; it's better to give than receive; and turn the other cheek."

But by far the most shocking statement Jesus ever made was when He declared, "I am the way and the truth and the life. No one comes to the Father, except through Me" (John 14:6, NIV). Today this statement still infuriates people like no other. Many consider it arrogant and narrow-minded. If you're seeking spiritual truths there may be something about this statement that bothers you deep down inside.

The Apostles recognized Jesus as God and the only pathway to God. John made this clear when he described Christ as "the Word" (John 1:1). Paul spoke of Jesus as the one who created all things and who holds all things together with His divine power (Colossians 1:16-17). He also addressed Jesus as "our great God and Savior, Jesus Christ" (Titus 2:13). The Bible is clear—Jesus not only claims to be God; but also that He is the only way to God. Take some time during your day and let this claim resonate in your heart and mind.

Point to Ponder: The most shocking statement Jesus ever made was the claim that He was God and the only pathway to eternal life. This exclusive assertion has been a stumbling block for many but salvation for those who believe.

Question to Consider: Why is it so difficult for people to believe that Jesus is the only way?

Most of us wonder if religious leaders aren't a bit like the three blind men asked to describe an elephant. One approached the beast, grabbed its trunk, and exclaimed confidently, "An elephant is long and tubular, capable of great contortions of shape." The second encountered the elephant, and after placing his hands on the animal's side said, "No, no, an elephant is very broad and leathery, hardly capable of bending at all." The third man grasped the elephant's tail and remarked with disgust, "You're both wrong. An elephant is quite thin and smooth with a wiry brush on the end."

These three men encountered the same elephant, and each came away with very different, even contradictory, views. Most people believe the same to be true of the relationship between different religions. These people say all religions have partial truths, but no one religion has the whole truth. At most, each religion grasps only a piece of the truth about the vastness of God.

Believing all religions are partially true and that none capture the whole truth can lead to viewing truth as relative. Without the standard of absolute truth, then what is true for you can be different than what is true for me. Truth becomes based not on fact but on whether or not you believe it—therefore leading to a belief in many pathways to God.

Yesterday we looked at a part of scripture where Jesus claimed to be the only way to God. In John 14:6, He says, "I am the way, and the truth, and the life. No one comes to the Father, but by Me."

With this one statement, Jesus boldly puts Christianity in a class by itself. Think about it. If the path to God is through Jesus, then Christianity cannot be reconciled with any other religion. Jesus was unique among the founders of world religions. Religions promote their teachings as the only way to God, but Jesus promoted Himself as the only way to God. This uniqueness of Christianity is rooted in the uniqueness of Jesus Himself. Simply and clearly, Jesus says to focus your life on Him.

Now you may be thinking, "If I focus on Jesus, He'll show me how to get nearer to God and give me some guiding principles and life-enhancing tips." No. Jesus says, "I am the way and the truth and the life. No one comes to the Father, except through Me." Make no mistake about it. Jesus is the pathway of life itself. Not a single soul gets close to God except through Him.

How do we know Jesus is who He says He is?

We know this by the way Jesus backs up His claim. Lee Strobel writes in his book, *The Case for Christ*, that Jesus validated His declaration of being God by fulfilling dozens of centuries-old prophecies that defy every mathematical odd. These prophecies were as unique as a fingerprint; one that only the Messiah could match, and in all of history, only Jesus has proven a perfect match.

One of the many prophecies that Jesus fulfilled was depicted in Mel Gibson's movie, *The Passion of the Christ*. When Judas betrayed Jesus by throwing thirty shekels of silver into the temple, it was the fulfillment of a prophecy made hundreds of years prior to the event.

Unlike other religious leaders, Jesus performed great miracles that further authenticated His claim of being God. The most spectacular demonstration of His deity occurred when Jesus fulfilled prophecy by being resurrected from the dead in a historical event witnessed by more than five hundred people.

Jesus didn't just say He was the one and only Son of God; He validated His claim like nobody else in history. He came to earth in human form to find you and lead you back to God. No other religion can point to a moment in history and say, "This is what God has done for you!" Remember, religion is our attempt to find God, but Christianity is God's attempt to find us. Think about it; God sent Jesus to lead us back to Himself.

This takes some pressure off of me. I don't have to perform in the right way, earn God's favor, or find a pathway to God. No, He makes it unmistakably clear that this pathway is based solely on what He already did for me. Jesus' life is the pathway to God, and God makes Jesus available to me. That's a big weight off my shoulders!

Jesus is unique! Friends, it really does matter which path you follow in your spiritual journey. Jesus' own words and life dispel the myth that all paths lead to God. So which path are you on, man's or God's?

Point to Ponder: Jesus does not give principles that help you find the way to God. Jesus is the way. He doesn't merely dispense truth. He is the truth. Jesus doesn't only talk about life. He is the life.

Question to Consider: What fulfilled prophecies validate the claim of Jesus to be the way, the truth, and the life?

If you genuinely believe something deep down in your soul without question or hesitation, does that make it true? I think most people would say no. We've all had a belief or two shattered somewhere along the line. Examples of this are belief in Santa Claus or the tooth fairy. Sorry if I've blown it for some of you holdouts. Others are more dramatically life-changing, like believing your parents will remain together forever only to later witness their painful separation and divorce.

One widely held belief is that sincere faith, regardless of the religion, will unlock the door to heaven. "It doesn't matter what you believe," some say, "as long as you're sincere about it." Does sincerity guarantee salvation? Take a look at some of these sincere beliefs and see what you think.

Religious sincerity is always related to a belief system.

> Mormon prophet Joseph Smith found a unique stone and sincerely believed that it was a seer stone. Staring at it intently, he believed he received a revelation that people of medium stature and a life span of nearly a thousand years inhabit the moon.

> Hindus sincerely believe that both human and animal spirits will reincarnate and return to earth many times in various life forms.

> After his death, followers of Confucius built a temple to honor him. They sincerely believed his spirit resided there, so they worshiped and offered sacrifices to it.

> Taoists sincerely believe that there are seven gods, and that Yu-huang is the god of gods to whom all other gods must report.

> Buddhists sincerely believe that a desire for existence perpetuates a cycle of successive reincarnations.

> Certain Muslim males sincerely believe that by sacrificing themselves to kill others, they'll gain possession of seventy-two sexually anxious, virgin females in paradise.

Sincere belief of a lie has tragic consequences.
What does God think of sincere believers who worship other gods? Let's take a look at one example recorded in 1 Kings 18.

A succession of ill-fated kings had brought Israel to an all-time low and Ahab, the evil king, was currently presiding with his corrupt queen, Jezebel. The living God is all but forgotten. Israel's popular gods were Baal, the storm god, and Asherah, the sex goddess. Not one to sit back while His people self-destructed, God sent Elijah to confront the king and deal with the worship of these pagan gods.

Ahab agreed to a face-off between his gods and the God of Elijah. On his side, Ahab gathered a huge crowd along with 850 so-called prophets of Baal and Asherah. Elijah confronted the crowd with a challenge: "If the Lord is God, follow him; but if Baal is God, follow him" (1 Kings 18:21, NIV). He then proposed a test to determine the true God. Each side would take its turn preparing an altar with firewood and a sacrifice. Elijah's altar was to God, and the other was an altar to Baal. "Call on the name of your Gods," said Elijah, "and I will call on the name of the Lord. The god who answers by fire—he is God" (1 Kings 18:24).

So the stage was set. First up, the prophets of Baal. All day long they raised their voices to Baal and expressed their devotion. They prayed loudly for an answer, but no fire came. Elijah mocked them, suggesting they try shouting louder as Baal might be in deep thought or away on a trip. They did, but still there was no fire.

Then it was Elijah's turn. He was so confident that he first drenched his altar with water before calling on God. "Then the fire of the Lord fell and burned up the sacrifice, the wood, the stones and the soil, and also licked up the water in the trench" (1 Kings 18:38). The prophets of Baal, revealed as frauds, were seized and executed.

Yes, belief in a lie has tragic consequences. A false religion is a lie conjured up by human imagination. Devotion to such is the ultimate human folly and one that leads to destruction.

Sincere belief in truth results in salvation and the certainty of heaven.
We began by looking at sincerity. Now let's take a look at truth. Webster defines truth as "that which accords with reality." Belief that a god whittled from wood decides your destiny, arsenic is health food, or that a coral snake is a dove simply doesn't accord with reality. The greater the sincerity of such beliefs, the greater the peril.

God places a high premium on truth and reality. Jesus identifies Himself as the personification of truth. "I am the way the truth and the life," He affirms. "No one comes to the Father except through Me" (John 14:6).

In stark contrast to false beliefs in man-made religions is Christ—who appeared among us, taught as no man could teach, performed miracles no man could perform, died for our sins, and validated His redemptive work on our behalf by His widely attested resurrection. Jesus Christ accords with reality. He is not a figment of human imagination, but a real historical person. He expects us to believe nothing without proof, and He proved beyond question the validity of His person, His message, and His mission, which was to suffer the penalty for human sin and save for eternity all those who trust in Him. Do you?

Point to Ponder: Sincerity will not make something true. A person can be sincerely wrong. Sincerity must align with truth to be affective. Therefore trust sincerely what is true, and reject sincerely what is false. Never rely on sincerity alone to lead the way.

Questions to Consider: What do you sincerely believe? Is it true? How do you know?

Many compassionate people have a difficult time accepting that believers of other religions will find themselves locked out of heaven. Why shouldn't Hindus, Confucianists, Shintoists, Zoroastrians, Muslims, and adherents of all religions, cults, and *isms* have a place in heaven? Who's to say that Christianity alone provides the exclusive key to eternal bliss?

The issue of Christ being the one and only way to heaven must be settled on fact, not wishful thinking or even empathy for others. One historical event distinguishes Christian faith from all religions. That fact is the resurrection of Jesus Christ. Aside from Christ, the bones of every founder of all religions throughout history are to this day in an earthly grave or tomb.

But the body of Jesus, confirmed dead by Roman crucifixion and placed in a well-guarded and heavily sealed rock tomb, is nowhere to be found. Three days after His burial, the tomb was discovered empty; at first, even His followers were dumbfounded. Then they began to recall Jesus' earlier predictions of both His death and resurrection (Matthew 16:21; Mark 9:31; Luke 18:33; John 10:17-18).

Evidence that Jesus Christ rose from the dead is beyond rational dispute. Dr. Simon Greenleaf is widely acclaimed as the greatest authority on legal evidence in the nineteenth century and has studied the eyewitness accounts of the resurrection of Christ. Why did he focus on the eyewitness accounts? Because eyewitness accounts are the most admissible evidence in any court of law ascertaining truth. In the end, he concluded the eyewitnesses in this case were notable for their integrity, ability, and truth. At least seventeen appearances of Christ after His resurrection are a part of the historical record. Take a look at some of the eyewitnesses Greenleaf studied.

> Mary Magdalene (John 20:11-17)

> The women (Matthew 28:9-10)

> Simon Peter (Luke 24:34)

> The disciples on the road to Emmaus (Mark 16:12-13)

> Eleven of the disciples (Mark 16:14)

> Eleven disciples a week after His resurrection (John 20:26-29)

> Seven disciples by the Sea of Galilee (John 21:1-23)

> More than five hundred people at one time (1 Corinthians 15:6)

> James, the Lord's brother (1 Corinthians 15:7)

> All of the disciples (1 Corinthians 15:7)

> Eleven apostles on a mountain in Galilee (Matthew 28:16-20)

> His disciples when He ascended from the Mount of Olives (Luke 24:44-53)

> Stephen, prior to his martyrdom (Acts 7:55-56)

> Paul on the road to Damascus (Acts 9:3-6)

> Paul in the temple (Acts 22:17-21)

> Paul in a Caesarea prison (Acts 23:11)

> The Apostle John on the Isle of Patmos (Revelation 1:12-20)

The record is clear and indisputable. Joseph of Arimathea placed Jesus' body in a tomb. Three days later, the tomb was found empty (Matthew 28:6). Witnesses to His resurrection were not waiting in expectation of Him; in fact, they were slow to comprehend what had happened (John 20:9-15). But once they realized He had conquered death, they and future generations of His followers have been willing to die rather than renounce Him. This is a profound reality. While many misled people have died for a lie, no person has been willing to die for a *known* lie.

Jesus Christ predicted His death and resurrection—He died, rose again, and personally appeared to hundreds of people. They were so convinced of His resurrection that the jaws of ravenous lions, the cross of crucifixion, a burning pyre, and the rack of torture could not dissuade them from following and serving Him. Does all of that really prove He is the only way to heaven? Let's consider the following.

1. The resurrection of Christ validates not only His person, but His teachings as well. Because He rose, we can rely on His message recorded in the Gospel of John. "Most assuredly I say to you, I am the door of the sheep. All who ever came before Me are thieves and robbers, but the sheep did not hear them. I am the door. If anyone enters by Me, he will be saved, and will go in and out and find pasture" (John 10:7-9, NKJV).

2. The resurrection of Christ proves He is not an impostor, but who He claimed to be—the divine Son of the Living God who affirmed, "I and My Father are one" (John 10:30, NKJV).

3. The resurrection of Christ authenticates the value of His redemptive work for lost people who place their faith in Him. It confirms that our justification before God is now accomplished (1 Corinthians 15:1-20; Romans 4:24).

4. The resurrection of Christ guarantees the resurrection of those who trust in Him (1 Corinthians 15:21-23).

5. The resurrection of Christ means He is our own source of power for Christian living, testimony, and service (Matthew 28:18; Ephesians 1:19-21).

6. The resurrection of Christ means He is now above all principality, power, and dominion—the living leader of the universal body of believers known as the church—the body of Christ (Ephesians 1:20-23).

7. The resurrection of Christ means God the Father has, "Begotten us again to a living hope…to an inheritance incorruptible and undefiled and that does not fade away, reserved in heaven for you" (1 Peter 1:3-4, NKJV).

Is Jesus the only way to heaven? That's what He claimed to be and His claims must be believed because He alone proved His deity by His resurrection from the dead. "I am the way, the truth, and the life. No one comes to the Father except through Me" (John 14:6, NKJV). He is the *Truth*, and truth cannot lie. He came not to found a religion, but to provide everlasting life for all those who trust in Him (John 3:16; 10:28). His resurrection proves His trustworthiness.

Point to Ponder: The most unique aspect of Christianity is that its leader died and rose from the dead. No other religion can make that claim. The resurrection of Jesus Christ is the most powerful and convincing argument that He really is the way, the truth, and the life.

Question to Consider: How does the resurrection of Jesus validate His claims?

My friend, Tom, believes that regardless of which religion you practice, we all end up in the same place. "Everyone will find his or her own way to God in the end," he says. "The Muslim in his way, the Hindu in her way, and the Christian in his way. How could God be so intolerant to allow only Christians into heaven?" Let's run with Tom's view for a moment and see where we end up.

One day I'm out walking and I meet another walker. We exchange greetings, and he mentions he's on a religious pilgrimage to The Little Chapel of the West. Now, I know the chapel is to the east of us and he's headed west, but I'm not going to rain on his religious parade. He's entitled to his opinion. And really, it's the journey that matters, not the destination.

This scenario is pretty ludicrous. In the name of tolerance, I'm doing this man a great disservice. Isn't this the same as Tom's perspective of a *tolerant* God? According to a recent poll by George Barna, 40 percent of American adults believe when Christians, Jews, Buddhists, and others pray to their god, they're all praying to the same god, but using different names for that deity.

Mahatma Gandhi of India would have agreed. He once said, "The soul of religion is one, but it is encased in a multitude of forms." Is this true? In actuality, the word *god* means different things within different religious frameworks.

> Hinduism says everything is God. You're God. I'm God. This book is God.

> Islam believes in Allah and his prophet Mohammed. It denies that Jesus is God and that He died for our sins.

> Buddhism is atheistic, believing there is no objective god or gods. At best, it's an agnostic religion believing there is no way of knowing. Buddha may not even have believed in God.

> Christianity says there's one eternal God who created the universe and exists as three persons: God the Father, God the Son, and God the Holy Spirit who came to earth as Jesus Christ, fully God and fully man.

Of all the world's major religions, Jesus is the only leader who claimed to be God in the flesh. Moses didn't. Mohammed didn't. Buddha didn't. Author C.S. Lewis wrote, "There is no parallel in other religions. If you had gone to Buddha and asked him, 'Are you the son of Bramah?' he would have said, 'My son, you are still in the vale of illusion.' If you had gone to Socrates and asked, 'Are you Zeus?' he would have laughed at you. If you had gone to Mohammed and asked, 'Are you Allah?' he would first rend his clothes and then cut off your head."

Dr. Michael Green is an internationally respected author, speaker, scholar, and is currently Senior Research Fellow at Wycliffe Hall, Oxford University. He recently authored the book, *But Don't All Religions Lead to God?* Navigating the Multi-Faith Maze (Baker Book House, 2002). Green wrote, "Perhaps the greatest difference of all [among religious views] lies in the Christian assertion that none of us can save ourselves and make ourselves acceptable to God...all the other faiths assert that by keeping their teachings a person will be saved, fulfilled, or reborn."

With the exception of Christianity, all religions have an established set of religious rites, commands, and ethical principles that, if followed, lead to salvation. Their human origins are evidenced in that salvation is humanly attainable.

In contrast, the Bible sets its moral and ethical standard as the very holiness and perfection of God Himself, demanding nothing less for salvation. No man would invent a standard so utterly impossible for man to achieve. Christ alone offers salvation by grace, received only through faith in Him. True Christianity is not a religion, but a person—Jesus Christ. He is the world's Creator and its only true Redeemer. "Neither is there salvation in any other: for there is none other name under heaven given among men, whereby we must be saved" (Acts 4:12, KJV).

People try to harmonize the religions of the world but there are drastic and irreconcilable differences between Christianity and other belief systems. Every other religion is based on trying to earn the favor of God. They are the attempts of humankind to reach out to God. But Jesus Christ is God reaching out to us. Do you see the difference?

Jesus taught the opposite of what other religions teach. He said we can't get to heaven of our own accord. We're all guilty of wrongdoing and it is what separates us from our holy and perfect God. Because God is a righteous judge, our wrongdoing has to be paid for. So out of His love, Jesus voluntarily offered Himself as our substitute to pay the penalty that we owed for our sin. When we receive His sacrifice, we are reunited with God for eternity.

This distinction is clearly demonstrated when comparing a parable taught by Jesus in the Bible with a similar story found in Buddhist literature. Both stories involve rebellious sons who left home, later recognized the error of their ways, and went back to be reconciled with their families. In the Buddhist story, the errant son must work off the penalty for his past misdeeds by spending years in servitude. But do you know how the Christian parable of the Prodigal Son ends? The repentant son is warmly welcomed home by his loving father and given undeserved grace and forgiveness.

Other religious leaders offer wise sayings and helpful insights, but none of them ever offered themselves as payment for our wrongdoing. Only Jesus Christ, the perfect Son of God, was qualified to sacrificially offer Himself as our substitute, paying the penalty for our sin, and guaranteeing salvation to all who come to Him. Now does that sound like an intolerant God?

Point to Ponder: Not all religions are the same. In fact, Christianity is distinct from all the rest. Every religion advocates a system of rules or principles for man to earn God's approval. The Christian gospels proclaim God's love and favor for all who believe.

Question to Consider: What are some additional differences between Christianity and other religions?

For many people, their belief in being able to gain entrance to heaven hinges on some form of their own goodness. Some might say, "I ought to make it because, unlike a lot of people I know, I'm a good person."

Many of the major religions of the world and too many Christ-followers hold the belief that goodness earns you a ticket to the best ride of all: heaven. But Christians who draw their understanding of salvation and heaven from the Bible disagree strongly with this idea. So what does the Bible say about this all-important question?

1. Sin is universal in the human race. "For all have sinned and fall short of the glory of God" (Romans 3:23). From Genesis to Revelation, the story of humankind is stained with human sin expressing itself in evil activity. Every one of the biblical words we've translated to our English word *sin* conveys the idea of rebellion against the will and purpose of God. Sin began in Eden (Genesis 3), and that sinful nature was passed on to all the generations that followed. All humans, with the single exception of Jesus Christ, who was God in human flesh, have been and are "by nature children of wrath" (Ephesians 2:3, NASB).

A human being is a fallen creature with a mind corrupted by sin (Romans 1:28), blinded by Satan (2 Corinthians 4:4), and gripped by a seared conscience (1 Timothy 4:2). Based on this, every member of the human race is born in sin (Psalm 51:5) and is sinful by nature (Ephesians 2:3). This includes people who believe themselves *good* enough to merit eternal bliss in heaven. This is an unrealistic, ill-founded, and unbiblical deception of hope.

2. Sin resulted in universal, spiritual death. "Therefore, just as through one man sin entered the world, and death through sin, and so death spread to all men, because all sinned" (Romans 5:12, NASB). Universal sin resulted in universal spiritual death—a condition scripture refers to as "dead in trespasses and sin" (Ephesians 2:1, NASB). Just as physical death separates the soul from the body, spiritual death separates the soul from God.

Jesus knew that humans, in their natural state, were spiritually dead. So He drove home the necessity of new birth to Nicodemus, the inquiring Pharisee. "Most assuredly, I say to you, unless one is born again, he cannot see the kingdom of God" (John 3:3, NKJV). The single greatest sentence in the Bible fell from the lips of our Savior, "For God so loved the world that He gave His only begotten Son, that whoever believes in Him should not perish, but have everlasting life" (John 3:16, NKJV). The only conceivable reason that people need life is because in our natural state, we do not have it. We are spiritually dead.

3. Salvation is not by goodness, but by grace. "In him we have redemption through his blood, the forgiveness of sins, in accordance with the riches of God's grace... For it is by grace you have been saved through faith—and this not from yourselves, it is the gift of God—not by works, so that no one can boast" (Ephesians 1:7; 2:8-9). Because our natural state leaves us spiritually dead, we lack the ability to save ourselves and gain entrance to heaven of our own accord. And so, motivated by infinite love, God took the initiative and extended His grace to us through Christ.

It was not through any goodness of ours that He acted on our behalf. As Paul said to Titus, "But when the kindness and the love of God our Savior toward man appeared, not by works of righteousness which we have done, but according to His mercy He saved us…that having been justified by His grace we should become heirs according to the hope of eternal life" (Titus 3:4-7, NKJV). Jesus gave this promise to all who trust in Him: "And I give them eternal life, and they shall never perish…" (John 10:28, NKJV).

Sadly, anyone devoted to man-made religions, cults, or any of the various *isms* that teach reliance on human goodness as a ticket to the ultimate ride of heaven, are deceived. We're all sinners unable to earn salvation by self-merit. Our only hope is to recognize our sinful nature, quit depending on our own goodness, and trust in Jesus Christ who acted on our behalf by taking on the just penalty for our sins. He freely and selflessly went to the cross and paid our debt, acting in love, mercy, and grace to save our very souls.

Human goodness is no ticket to heaven; but make no mistake, goodness characterizes the life of a true Christian. Not only do we get the gift and security of salvation and eternal life through faith in Christ, we also get to host residence to the Holy Spirit (1 Corinthians 3:16, 6:19). "The fruit of the Spirit is love, joy, peace, longsuffering, kindness, goodness, faithfulness, gentleness, self control" (Galatians 5:22-23, NKJV). We are "a new creation" in Christ. "Old things have passed away; behold, all things have become new" (2 Corinthians 5:17, NKJV).

Goodness and service pleasing to God flows naturally from a regenerated and forever-grateful Christian life. Goodness is not a means of salvation, but the result of it, showing up in the conduct of anyone who has accepted the gift of eternal life. The assurance of heaven by faith in Christ changes us into different people who manifest the fruit of the indwelling Holy Spirit, including goodness.

Your ticket to heaven, my friend, was already signed, sealed, and delivered long before your birth by the loving, gracious sacrifice of the Son of God. All you have to do is accept the ticket.

Point to Ponder: Sin is universal and extends to everyone. Therefore the potential to be good enough to get to heaven does not exist. It is only by God's grace that we can have salvation. Grace is greater than all our sin.

Question to Consider: Why is goodness the result of salvation but not the means to achieve it?

The following are selected works for further study. They are categorized as beginner (B), intermediate (I), and advanced (A) as far as their depth of study. Those marked with an asterisk (*) are highly recommended.

Week One: Why Am I Here?

* Beckwith, Francis J., Craig, William Lane, & Moreland, J.P. *To Everyone An Answer: The Case For the Christian Worldview*. Downers Grove: InterVarsity Press, 2004. (I)

* Boyd, Gregory A. *Letters From A Skeptic*. Colorado Springs: Chariot Victor Publishing, 1994. (B)

* Boa, Ken & Moody, Larry. *I'm Glad You Asked*. Colorado Springs: Chariot Victor Publishing,1994. (B)

Copan, Paul. *That's Just Your Interpretation*. Grand Rapids: Baker Book House, 2001. (B)

Craig, William Lane, *Reasonable Faith*. Wheaton: Crossway Books, 1994. (I)

Geisler, Norman L. & Hoffman, Paul K. *Why I am a Christian*. Grand Rapids: Baker Book House, 2001. (B)

Knechtle, Cliffe. *Give Me an Answer*. Downers Grove: InterVarsity Press, 1986. (B)

Kreeft, Peter & Tacelli, Ronald K. *Pocket Handbook of Christian Apologetics*. Downers Grove: InterVarsity Press, 2003. (B)

* Little, Paul E. *Know Why You Believe*, 4th Edition. Downers Grove: InterVarsity Press, 2000. (B)

*Little, Paul E. *How To Give Away Your Faith*. Downers Grove: InterVarsity Press, 1988. (B)

*Moreland, J.P. *Scaling the Secular City*. Grand Rapids: Baker Book House, 1987. (I)

* Strobel, Lee. *The Case For Faith*. Grand Rapids: Zondervan, 2000. (B)

* Warren, Rick. *The Purpose Driven Life*. Grand Rapids: Zondervan, 2002. (B)

Web Sites

http://www.str.org/ - Stand To Reason…a Christian organization led by Greg Koukl with multiple resources on topics and questions relevant to Christianity. This website also has excellent links to other great resources.

http://www.rizm.org - RZIM…the international ministry of Ravi Zacharias. The Web site includes many downloadable talks/lectures relative to the subjects discussed in week one.

Week Two: Why Should I Believe in God in the First Place?

* Craig, William Lane & Sinnott-Armstrong, Walter. *God? A Debate Between A Christian And An Atheist*. New York: Oxford University Press, 2004. (A)

Ganssle, Gregory E. *Thinking About God*. Downers Grove: InterVarsity Press, 2004. (I)

Lewis, C.S. *Mere Christianity*. New York: Simon and Schuster, 1943, rev. ed. 1952. (B)

Poole, Garry. *How Does Anyone Know God Exists? Tough Questions,* Revised Edition. Grand Rapids: Zondervan, 2003. (B)

* Strobel, Lee. *The Case for a Creator*. Grand Rapids: Zondervan, 2004. (B)

Vitz, Paul C. *Faith of the Fatherless: The Psychology of Atheism*. Dallas: Spence Publishing, 1999. (I)

* Zacharias, Ravi. *Can Man Live Without God*. Dallas: Word Publishing, 1994. (I)

Week Three: Why Should I Trust the Bible?

* Barnett, Paul. *Is the New Testament Reliable?* Downers Grove: InterVarsity Press, 1986. (B)

Bruce, F.F. *The New Testament Documents: Are They Reliable?* Grand Rapids: Eerdmans, 2003. (B)

Geisler, Norman L. & Nix, William E. *A General Introduction to the Bible.* Chicago: Moody Press, 1986. (I)

Patzia, Arthur G. *The Making of the New Testament.* Downers Grove: InterVarsity Press, 1995. (B)

Poole, Garry. *How Reliable is the Bible? Tough Questions* Revised Edition. Grand Rapids: Zondervan, 2003. (B)

* Sheler, Jeffery L. *Is The Bible True?* San Francisco: HarperCollins, 1999. (I)

* Witherington III, Ben. *The New Testament Story*. Grand Rapids: Eerdmans, 2004. (B)

Week Four: Why Is the World So Messed Up?

Blocher, Henri. *Evil and the Cross*. Downers Grove: InterVarsity Press, 1990. (B)

* Boyd, Gregory A. *Is God to Blame?* Downers Grove: InterVarsity Press, 2003. (B)

* Boyd, Gregory A. *Satan And The Problem of Evil*. Downers Grove: InterVarsity Press, 2003. (A)

Lewis, C.S. *The Problem of Pain*. San Francisco: HarperCollins, 1940, HarperCollins ed., 2001. (I)

Poole, Garry. *How Could God Allow Suffering and Evil? Tough Questions* Revised Edition. Grand Rapids: Zondervan, 2003. (B)

* Sittser, Gerald L. *A Grace Disguised: How the Soul Grows Through Loss.* Grand Rapids, Zondervan, 1995. (B)

* Stackhouse, John G. *Can God Be Trusted?* New York: Oxford University Press, 1998. (I)

Week Five: Why the Conflict...Science and the Bible?

* Behe, Michael J. *Darwin's Black Box.* New York: The Free Press, 1997. (A)

Dembski, William A., ed. *Mere Creation: Science, Faith & Intelligent Design.* Downers Grove: InterVarsity Press, 1998. (I)

Dembski, William A. ed. *Uncommon Dissent*, Wilmington: ISI Books, 2004. (A)

Dembski, William A. *Intelligent Design.* Downers Grove: InterVarsity Press, 1999. (I)

Denton, Michael. *Evolution: A Theory In Crisis*. Bethesda: Adler & Adler, 1985. (A)

* Johnson, Phillip E. *Darwin On Trial*. Washington D.C.: Regnery Gateway, 1991 (I)

Johnson, Phillip E. *Defeating Darwinism*. Downers Grove: InterVarsity Press, 1997. (B)

Moreland, J.P., ed. *The Creation Hypothesis.* Downers Grove: InterVarsity Press, 1994. (I)

* Moreland, J.P., and John Mark Reynolds, eds. *Three Views On Creation And Evolution.* Grand Rapids: Zondervan, 1999. (B)

Poole, Garry. *Do Science and the Bible Conflict? Tough Questions,* Revised Edition. Grand Rapids: Zondervan, 2003. (B)

Web Sites

http://www.arn.org/ - Access Research Network...This Web site focuses on the intelligent design movement.

http://www.discovery.org/csc/ - Discovery Institute (Center for Science and Culture)...This Web site also focuses on the intelligent design movement.

Week Six: Why Jesus?

Anderson, Sir Norman. *Christianity and World Religions.* Downers Grove: InterVarsity Press, 1984. (B)

Copan, Paul & Tacelli, Ronald K. (Eds.) *Jesus' Resurrection: Fact or Figment?* Downers Grove: InterVarsity Press, 1999. (I)

* Koukl, Gregory. *Jesus The Only Way* (100 verses) Stand to Reason Perspective Series, 1995. (B)

Okholm, Dennis L. & Phillips, Timothy R. (Eds.) *Four Views On Salvation In A Pluralistic World.* Grand Rapids: Zondervan, 1996. (I)

Poole, Garry. *What Difference Does Jesus Make? Tough Questions,* Revised Edition. Grand Rapids: Zondervan, 2003. (B)

* Strobel, Lee. *The Case For Christ.* Grand Rapids: Zondervan, 1998. (B)

* Wilkins, Michael J. & Moreland, J.P., (Eds.) *Jesus Under Fire.* Grand Rapids: Zondervan, 1995. (I)

Wright, N.T. *The Challenge of Jesus.* Downers Grove: InterVarsity Press, 1999. (I)

* Wright, N.T. *The Resurrection and the Son of God.* Minneapolis: Fortress Publishing, 2003. (A)

* Zacharias, Ravi. *Jesus Among Other Gods.* Nashville: Word Publishing, 2000. (I)

1. Quoted in Gerald R. McDermott, *Seeing God* (Downers Grove, IL: InterVarsity Press, 1995), 136.

2. Cited in Terry L. Miethe, *Living Your Faith* (Joplin: College Press, 1993), 24.

3. http://freethought.freeservers.com/reason/faith.html

4. Paul E. Little, *Know Why You Believe* (Downers Grove, IL: InterVarsity Press, 1988), 13.

5. Carl Sagan, *Cosmos* (New York: Random House, 1980), 4.

6. Quoted by Lee Strobel, *The Case For A Creator* (Grand Rapids: Zondervan, 2004), 74-75.

7. Strobel, *The Case For A Creator*, 75.

8. Robert Jastrow, *Until the Sun Dies* (New York: W.W. Norton, 1977)

9. Chuck Colson & Nancy Pearcey, *How Now Shall We Live* (Wheaton: Tyndale, 1999), 58.

10. Robert Jastrow, *God and the Astronomers* (New York: W.W. Norton, 1978), 116.

11. Debate on the existence of God, see http://www.leaderu.com/offices/billcraig/docs/craig-pigliucci0.html

12. David Quammen, *National Geographic*, Was Darwin Wrong? November 2004.

13. K.R. Miller and J. Levine, *Biology* (Englewood Cliffs: Prentice Hall, 1995), 658.

14. J.P. Moreland, *Scaling the Secular City* (Grand Rapids: Baker Book House, 1987), 220.

15. Sir Frederick Hoyle, *The Intelligent Universe* (London: Michael Joseph, 1983), 251.

16. Phillip E. Johnson, *Darwin On Trial* (Washington, D.C.: Regnery Gateway, 1991), 36–37.

17. Lee Strobel, *The Case for a Creator* (Grand Rapids: Zondervan, 2004), 193.

18. Foreward to the 100th anniversary edition of Darwin's book, *Origin of Species* in 1959.

19. John S. Feinberg, *No One Like Him* (Wheaton: Crossway Books, 2001), 571.

20. Paul Copan, *That's Just Your Interpretation* (Grand Rapids: Baker Book House, 2001), 146–52.

21. Copan, 147.

22. (Ed.) J.P. Moreland, *The Creation Hypothesis* (Downers Grove: InterVarsity Press, 1994),11.

23. Whole books have been dedicated to these matters; we highly recommend...Moreland, J.P. & Reynolds, John Mark, *Three Views on Creation and Evolution*. Grand Rapids: Zondervan, 1999.

24. Gordon J. Wenham, *Genesis 1–15, Vol. 1* (Dallas: Word, 1987).

25. John S. Feinberg, *No One Like Him* (Wheaton: Crossway Books,2001), 599.

26. Feinberg, *No One Like Him*, 597.

27. English Standard Version

28. J.P. Moreland and John Mark Reynolds, eds., *Three Views On Creation And Evolution* (Grand Rapids: Zondervan, 1999), 268.

29. Richard Dawkins, *The Blind Watchmaker* (New York: Norton & Company, 1986), 5.

30. J.P. Moreland and John Mark Reynolds, eds., *Three Views On Creation And Evolution* (Grand Rapids: Zondervan, 1999), 275.

31. William A. Dembski, ed., *Mere Creation: Science, Faith & Intelligent Design* (Downers Grove: InterVarsity Press, 1998), 93–94.

32. William A. Dembski, *Intelligent Design* (Downers Grove: InterVarsity Press, 1999), 106.

33. Norman L. Geisler, *Baker Encyclopedia of Christian Apologetics* (Grand Rapids: Baker Book House, 1999), 26.

34. Geisler, *Baker Encyclopedia of Christian Apologetics*, 26.